Building

D0388862

Knowledge-Based Culture

Using Twenty-first Century Work and Decision-Making Systems in Associations

Principal Authors

Glenn H. Tecker, Kermit M. Eide, Jean S. Frankel

Contributing Authors

Bud E. Crouch, Irving J. Tecker, John A. Tucillo

Research and Development Team

Elaine Kotell Binder, Catherine D. Bower, Heather J. Campbell, Larry N. Garfield, Kathy L. Griggs, Patricia Walker Hickmann, Beth E. Kuna, Grace McGartland, H. B. Scoggins, Laura M. Shea

American Society of Association Executives

The authors have worked to ensure that all information in this book is accurate as of the time of publication and consistent with standards of good practice in the general management community. As research and practice advance, however, standards may change. For this reason it is recommended that readers evaluate the applicability of any recommendations in light of particular situations and changing standards.

Figures and tables in this book are copyrighted by Tecker Consultants. These may not be duplicated in any way without the express permission of the authors.

Director of book publishing, Linda H. Munday
Editor, Patricia L. Poupore
Designer, Keith A. Dana

Library of Congress Cataloging-in-Publication Data

Tecker, Glenn H.

Building a knowledge-based culture: Using twenty-first century work and decision-making systems in associations/principle authors, Glenn Tecker, Kermit Eide, Jean Frankel; contributing authors, Bud Crouch . . . (et al.); research and development team, Elaine Binder . . . (et al.).

p. cm.

ISBN 0-88034-130-0

1. Associations, institutions, etc.—Information services—Management. 2. Nonprofit organizations—Information services—Management. 3. Decision support systems. I. Frankel, Jean (Jean Stark), 1957- . II. Eide, Kermit (Kermit Maurice), 1945- . III. American Society of Association Executives. IV. Title.
HV41.T44 1997 97-17805
366'.0068—dc21 CIP

Copyright ©1997 by the American Society of Association Executives. All rights reserved. The text portions of this work may not be reproduced or transmitted in any form or any means, electronic or mechanical, including photocopying, recording, or by an information retrieval system without permission in writing from the publisher.

American Society of Association Executives
1575 Eye Street, N.W.
Washington, D.C. 20005-1168

Printed in the United States of America

Discounts of ASAE books are available. For information, contact ASAE at (202)626-2723.

Contents

Foreword

The ASAE Foundation, in cooperation with the American Society of Association Executives, is dedicated to enhancing the future effectiveness of the association community.

This book is the result of a grant investment made by the ASAE Foundation, matched by resources from Tecker Consultants, Inc., to help association executives manage their associations successfully in the future. Tecker and his colleagues have investigated the elements of knowledge-based decision making, the organizational culture that supports these efforts, and the changes in governance needed to move forward to a competitive, successful future.

Their argument is persuasive. Every association executive can benefit from a thorough understanding of the principles and practices of knowledge-based organizational management, with the ultimate result of serving their members in a more customized, timely, and targeted manner.

The board of directors of the ASAE Foundation is grateful to the host of contributors to the Endowing the Future capital campaign. Without their investment in the future of association management, the research and creation of new knowledge captured here would not have been possible.

James P. Evans
1996-1998 ASAE Foundation Chair
Executive Vice President of Operations,
Doubletree Hotels Corporation

Preface

This book is intended to encourage a dialogue about issues involved in initiating and sustaining a journey that we believe that no association has yet fully completed. It offers an overview of the organizational competencies not-for-profit enterprises will need to succeed in the twenty-first century. It discusses an approach to re-focusing organizational structures, processes, and cultures that has not yet been fully achieved by even the most successful of today's leading associations.

It examines a new model of operational philosophy for associations that is significantly different in many important ways from the approaches that bring success today. It suggests a kind of commitment that will require some associations to significantly modify current practices, some to leap ahead over their own current best practices, and still others to abandon much of their histories to achieve new positioning for the future.

The character of the future environments of associations and of the association community is still emerging. No amount of research—statistical, empirical, or anecdotal—can project with great confidence the nature of tomorrow's demands and opportunities.

Like the great democratic experiment that spawned the North American model of associations, the greatest strength of the operational approach examined in this text may be that it assumes the need for continual adaptation. As important, the means for nimble adjustment is built into it.

The concepts and insights shared here have evolved from several years of actively assisting associations in shaping themselves and their members' futures. They have been tested both by reality and by thoughtful consideration by hundreds of association leaders who have participated in American Society for Association Executive's Symposium for chief staff and elected leaders over the past seven years. In fact, the constant requests of those participants for a non-technical text examining the issues discussed in those symposia stimulated the research and writing effort that produced this book.

These participants suggested the need to author text that would not be mistaken for an argument for a particular model, structure, or process. They suggested such a book should not even be an adaptable template designed to be customized by an association in search of "the answer" from someone else. They indicated that a "portrait" of the things they would need to attend to and a discussion of the issues they would most likely encounter would be most valuable.

This book is a product of two years of case study research, anecdotal validation, empirical experimentation, reinvestigation, expert analysis, and educated guessing. In a very real way, this publication reports on a "work in progress." It is dedicated to the many pioneering association leaders—both staff and members—who are demonstrating foresight and courage and delivering practical outcomes while fashioning a future for the communities of common interest they serve.

The issues involved in becoming knowledge based are likely to be similar across most associations. Taking the journey to a knowledge-based operational philosophy and the behavioral culture that enables it, however, inherently requires each organization that undertakes it to thoughtfully discern its own unique path and picture. We hope you and your organization will benefit from this reading.

Glenn H. Tecker
Kermit M. Eide
Jean S. Frankel

Introduction

Our members have told us they want access to a broad range of content, presented in an engaging way, easy-to-use, affordably priced, and with a strong sense of community. These factors are the underpinnings of our success, because our members have, in turn, brought other members . . .

This thought came not from an association executive, but from Steve Case, the president of America On-Line (AOL), one of the leading on-line services. Despite its infamous service woes in recent months, AOL, in its provision of information, education, forums for discussion, and advocacy of on-line freedom of speech, has become a virtual association. With its ease of access and low-cost point of entry, it is competing head on with the association as an institution for the dwindling free time and interest of both members and prospective members. With its advocacy, education, and other member services, AOL can be considered not just a virtual community, but a "virtual association," representing a very non-traditional, yet significant, competitive threat to many associations.

It is now clear that associations in the twenty-first century will need to be very different than they are today. They will require the ability to not only meet the rapidly changing expectations of an increasingly segmented membership community, but to challenge new sources of competition for the time and energy of that membership, to harness technology as a strategic advantage, to anticipate the future, and to position for change. They will need to do this by effectively transforming data into knowledge and by integrating that knowledge into their organization's strategies, processes, culture, and operational philosophy. They will need to adopt what is referred to here as a knowledge-based operational philosophy.

Internet Time

The current environment certainly presents significant challenges as well. The velocity of change is increasing at a frightening pace. The amount of information that technology has enabled us to choose from for our decision-making processes has surpassed overload status. Indeed, we are living, as the phrase was coined in *Business Week* in July 1996, in "Internet time," which, in its ability to bring us vast amounts of information at a rapid pace, is synonymous with living in dog years, in which seven times as many events happen for every one year.

For associations, as for their counterparts in the private sector, technology and the information tidal wave has truly become a two-edged sword. On one hand, it enables non-traditional competitors to easily serve an association's members. On the other, it holds unprecedented promise for a myriad of new and innovative methods for associations to serve their members more effectively. The challenges are clear: how can associations continue to be successful, for example, in providing research and information to their members, when their members can now access that information directly on the Internet?

The answer is also clear: associations must become the key navigators of information for their members. They must provide a pathway to help them select the most critical data based on the association's unique understanding of their members' needs, wants, and expectations. They must capitalize on an evolved knowledge base about the members, professions, and industries they serve. They must represent significant value to their members. They must embrace a methodology that, in a phrase, moves them from providers of data and information to resources of knowledge. This book attempts to navigate its readers toward an understanding and embracing of the philosophies, cultures, practices, and tools that are likely to support such transformations in a not-for-profit enterprise.

Success in this new competitive landscape (that is here to stay) will require the ability to constantly scan the horizon for the best and most relevant and meaningful information available—that information that will enable us to provide "value added" for our members, our staffs, and ourselves—and the ability to turn that information into knowledge.

It will require constant reshaping of our organizational cultures, structures, and outlooks as we become knowledge based. In a knowledge-based organization, who makes decisions will not be nearly as important as the quality of information on which decisions are made. This book will focus on becoming a knowledge-based decision-making association as an operational philosophy.

Organizations must access their historic and current operational philosophies and define what will be needed in the future. Reshaping an association to be knowledge-based is not just about information and technology; it is about relationships and culture as well.

Using This Book Effectively

This book is often provocative. This is not because it is argumentative, but because it frequently ventures into the still unknown or uncertain.

It is intended to be a conversation about what is involved in building a knowledge-based operational culture. This culture is based on a philosophy that institutionalizes a consultative partnership between staff and elected leaders. In such a partnership, both parties exchange insight and believe that the synergy of their different, but equally valuable, contributions leads to the organization's success. This culture promotes decision making based on purpose, policy, strategy, and considered perspective, rather than on politics, power plays, personalities, or perception of the moment.

These pages identify the kinds of things that need to be considered within associations that believe, as we do, that a knowledge-based approach is a prerequisite to sustaining success into the twenty-first century. This is intended as a handbook for anyone in a position to architect, influence, or participate in the management and dissemination of knowledge in an association. It usefully blends real experience and practical advice. It is equally relevant for the association's executives, chief elected officer, and colleagues on the organization's governing board, as well as for staff and volunteer leaders.

This book discusses and describes:

1. What it means to become knowledge based and why it is important
2. An understanding of the essential elements and considerations involved in becoming knowledge based
3. A framework for organizational strategies designed to prepare an association for deploying knowledge-based operational philosophies

Read this text in whole or in parts, at one time or over a period of time. Chapters are titled and organized to enable you to go back to germane parts for later reference or to stimulate thought.

There is no clear, critical path or linear sequence to the topics considered here, as is traditional with more academic treatises. The work involved in developing and sustaining a knowledge-based philosophy does not involve the execution of a template of carefully ordered steps, implemented according to some checklist or formula. Achieving a knowledge-based approach involves a variety of tangible and intangible actions, often conducted in parallel timelines with undetermined end points.

CHAPTER 1

Overview of the "Knowledge-Based" Operational Model

A knowledge-based operational philosophy does not just involve acquiring and distributing data. It involves building and sustaining an organization where individuals and groups, at all levels, actually use information routinely in decision making.

Operating with Informed Intuition

Creating, assembling, engineering, interpreting, and distributing information is what successful associations have historically done well. However, the rapid and increasingly unpredictable change that already characterizes the twenty-first century will require associations to move beyond data base management to a culture that pursues informed intuition.

Informed intuition is accessed by considering the implications of four interrelated perspectives or knowledge bases:

1. Sensitivity to member needs, expectations, and preferences
2. Foresight into the likely evolution of the environment in which members live
3. Insight into the capacity and strategic position of the organization
4. Consideration of the ethical dimensions of choices

When informed intuition is developed, used, stored, and shared among decision makers and workers, an association is better able to maintain appropriate balance in focus between (1) the momentum produced by coherency in direction and (2) the responsiveness to opportunity enabled by flexibility.

When intelligently considered, defensible information is carefully blended with expert and user instincts about the future, and when this combination is consistently expected to be used in making decisions, the organization is operating with informed intuition. It is this expectation that institutionalizes a consultative partnership between staff and members. Staff and members, in such a relationship, can direct their attention to keeping a balanced focus between maintaining momentum and seizing emerging opportunities. When this can be accomplished, leadership has positioned

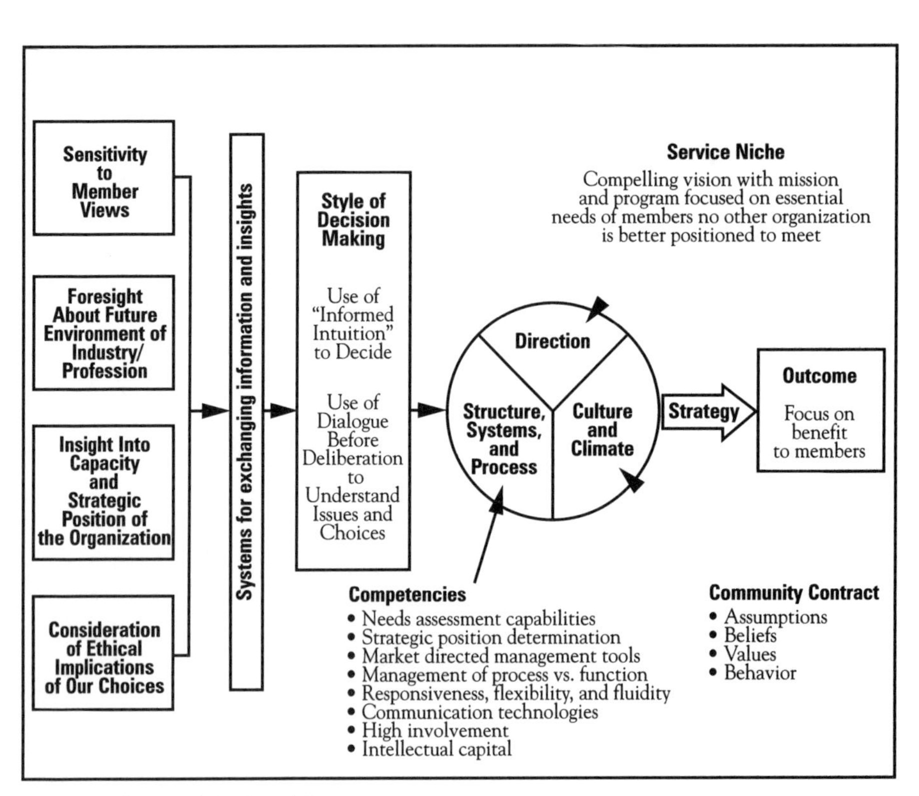

Figure 1. The Knowledge-Based Organization

the association to take full advantage of the knowledge-based operational philosophy tomorrow will demand.

A Transactional Enterprise

A knowledge-based association is a transactional enterprise. The primary currency of those transactions is information and insight.

Knowledge-based decision making involves:

- considering the four interrelated perspectives (and the kinds of information needed to inform those considerations) in any significant decision;

- exchanging knowledge and insights among study, decision, and work groups; and
- conducting a style of decision making that emphasizes informed intuition and employs dialogue before deliberation.

The character of a knowledge-based organization is shaped by three key attributes:

1. A *sense of direction* enabled by clarity and consensus on what will constitute success. This direction is reflected in a service niche driven by a compelling vision that is supported by a mission and program focused on essential member needs the association is well positioned to meet.
2. *Systems, structures, and processes* that promote functioning in ways that support effectiveness and efficiency.
3. *Culture and climate* based on beliefs, assumptions, and values that encourage behavior compatible with the kind of work required to achieve desired outcomes.

In the culture of knowledge-based, not-for-profit organizations, *who* makes the decision will not be nearly as important as the quality of the information on which decisions are made. Rational, common data bases will be developed and maintained to guide decisions about programs, policies, strategies, and delivery systems. Organizations will make a habit of securing information on an ad hoc basis when it is necessary and relevant to important emerging issues. Members and staffs, at all levels, will be engaged in continuous and integrated considerations of: (1) member wants, needs, and preferences, (2) capacity and strategic position of organizations, (3) external marketplace dynamics and realities, and (4) fairness and appropriateness of choices.

Decisions, at all levels, will be premised on careful consideration of the answers, as they are best known at the time, to four critical questions:

1. What is known about member, prospective member, and customer wants, needs, and preferences that is relevant to this decision?
2. What is known about the capacity and strategic position of the organization that is relevant to this decision?
3. What is known about the current realities and evolving dynamics of members' marketplace, industry, and profession that is relevant to this decision?
4. What are the ethical implications of these choices?

Eight Fundamental Competencies

The knowledge-based operational philosophy is evolving from tomorrow's leading associations through their efforts to build on eight fundamental competencies. The effective execution and integration of these competencies requires and promotes a very different kind of culture. These competencies follow below.

1. *Needs Assessment Capabilities*—This involves developing and maintaining a rational, common data base to guide decisions about member wants, needs, and preferences—including (1) demographic, qualitative, and quantitative information about member (and customer) expectations of a product's or service's ability to solve a problem or provide a valued benefit, (2) timely delivery of services, (3) value pricing, (4) reliability, and (5) service responsiveness. It also involves the ability of developers and decision makers at all levels to constantly access useful information and consider it in their work.

2. *Strategic Position Determination*—This competency requires tracking and assessment processes that include: (1) analyzing competition (anything that meets specific member needs, not just other associations); (2) assessing external dynamics and realities; (3) reaching consensus on desired outcomes (goals); (4) realistically appraising the match between core capabilities and desired outcomes, strategies, and business lines; and (5) identifying opportunities and developing alternative responses to those opportunities.

3. *Market-Directed Management Tools*—A balanced use should be made of all the tools of market-directed management: strategic planning, marketing research and assessment (both formal and informal), and sales, promotion, and membership development. This competency also involves strict accountability of products and services to fulfilling defined factors of success in effectiveness and financial contribution.

4. *Management of Process Versus Function*—This competency involves using teams across functions to manage processes and eliminate delays and bottlenecks, and it involves developing systems that support work processes. It also involves using viable systems and tools fostering continuous improvement of operations and products and services with the commitment of all involved.

5. *Responsiveness, Flexibility, and Fluidity*—This is achieved by reducing time between identifying a need or opportunity and taking real action that creates benefit. It involves compressing timelines by eliminating wait time between decisions or steps in work, or aggregating related work from different groups without decreasing involvement or abandoning appropriate accountability.

6. *Communication Technologies*—This involves providing opportunities for input and review without gathering for face-to-face meetings at a single site and increasing the timely use of knowledge (usefully applied information) in decision making at all levels of the organization.

7. *High Involvement*—This is demonstrated by (1) using ad hoc groups of experts and representatives of key stakeholder groups to address complex issues; (2) increasing empowerment and use of staff to do "real" work with a complementary partnership with members to give direction, to guide and advise, and to review and revise; and (3) reduced dependency on hierarchical structures for review and approval.

8. *Intellectual Capital*—Intellectual capital is both a platform and a prerequisite framework for knowledge-based decision making. The other seven fundamentals all depend on the sufficiency and appropriateness of the association's collective intelligence.

Using intellectual capital to its fullest possible advantage involves:

1. *Defining the role of knowledge:*
   a) In the organization
   b) In the relevant part of the industry
   c) For members

2. *Competitive assessment*
   This refers to assessing "uniqueness" of the knowledge. What knowledge does the organization possess/have access to that others (competitors) do not? What is your "knowledge niche?"

3. *Evaluation*
   What are your knowledge assets worth? What do they cost? What will it take to maximize their value? (Note: This is an important step to justify the investment.)

4. *Investing*
   Identify gaps you must fill and investments you must make to exploit knowledge—research and development, technology, processes, structures needed, etc.

5. *Assembling and repeating process*
   Organize your knowledge portfolio, and repeat the process continuously.

Community Contract

The culture of a knowledge-based association will include *assumptions and beliefs* (its view of the world); *values* (what it considers most important in that world); and

Table 1. Traditional and Knowledge-Based Cultures

Leadership Differences

Traditional Values	Knowledge-Based Values
• We take pride in making good decisions • We manage attention, meaning, trust, and self	• We take pride in seeing that good decisions are made • Informed intuition is acceptable • We use the process of knowledge and insight creation to manage attention, meaning, trust, and self • We create an environment supporting and promoting behaviors needed to be knowledge based • We use a facilitative model of decision making

Resource Allocation Differences

Traditional Values	Knowledge-Based Values
• It is better to miss an opportunity than to make a mistake • We will never have enough resources to do what needs to be done properly • We don't really have to lead the industry; we're only an association	• Reallocating resources can make a difference • We are not just seeking increased efficiency, but seeking to add value • Doing the right thing does not necessarily require great resources • We cannot afford to not get started if we're dealing with a strategically important issue • We have a great amount of intellectual capital that is not being fully and effectively used • We must uncover opportunities and better allocate available resources

Differences in What the Association Rewards

Traditional Values	Knowledge-Based Values
• We do lots of activities • We take time to deliberate; consensus is more important than expediency • Pay your dues in the association; put in your time to move ahead and be chosen to participate • Express your opinions eloquently • We reward loyalty and hard work	• We achieve results and outcomes • It is acceptable to articulate what you are thinking and why • Past leaders form part of the intellectual capital on which the association can draw and are valued for their expertise, not because they are part of a group of past presidents • We apply the correct combination of relevant experience to the issue or challenge • We think critically and analytically; people are chosen to participate in issues based on these abilities more than whether they have already paid their dues

Table 1. Traditional and Knowledge-Based Cultures *(continued)*

Enfranchisement/Representation Differences	
Traditional Values	**Knowledge-Based Values**
• Belonging (enfranchisement) is constituency based; I'm represented, therefore I am • One's ability to navigate the political system is valued • Authority comes from the support and size of the constituency, not knowledge	• There is no need for being physically represented by someone in your constituency if there is real and meaningful opportunity to communicate issues/concerns (e.g., send and receive important information); *I have an open channel for communication, therefore I am* • Validation can occur through communication, not necessarily direct representation • Authority is based on what you know and can bring • People are valued for the ideas and insight they bring to dialogue and problem solving

Differences in Communication/Stories/Myths	
Traditional Values	**Knowledge-Based Values**
• Association leaders are responsible for influencing the beliefs and behaviors of others • Avoid a mistake • Members have a responsibility to tell the association what they want • There will be some who will oppose us; the more they know, the more arguments they will be able to make against our position • We effectively use constituency power • There is a tendency to hold information; *We don't know everything about the issue yet, so we need to wait until we can figure out the answer*	• We engage in open dialogue before deliberating or decision making • The more people/members know, the more insight, opportunities, and challenges they will be able to help us see • Individuals are responsible for their own behavior if they have been given relevant information • The association is responsible for determining what members will need • We share what we know and believe others may participate in creating solutions/responses • We talk about the learning community: us • We make effective use of insight and information

behaviors (how it acts based on those shared opinions) that may differ significantly from some of the traditional views historically present in an association. Some traditional elements of the historic culture are likely to be congruent with the knowledge-based approach. These elements of the organization's tradition will be preserved and sustained. Movement toward a more knowledge-based philosophy does not necessarily require abandoning all traditions, practices, and sources of pride. As the overall organizational profile of the association transitions to a more knowledge-based approach, the mix of historic and new values will change and create a new cultural portrait.

What would a person observe as different in an association culture that was increasingly knowledge based? Differences in culture are likely to be most apparent in five key areas: (1) leadership, (2) resource allocation, (3) what the organization rewards, (4) enfranchisement/representation, and (5) communication/stories/myths. These areas serve only as examples; they are not a comprehensive list of differences or a most desirable portrait.

Based on these five key areas, table 1 illustrates the kinds of differences in the work world of a knowledge-based association from that of a more traditional or typical association. This does not constitute a complete picture or two columns of mutually contradictory traits.

These cultural profiles have been valuable to associations for considering (1) which traditional values are strengths, compatible with a knowledge-based commitment, that they wish to preserve and build on; and (2) which beliefs, assumptions, values, and behaviors of a more knowledge-based environment are attractive additions or substitutions.

Service Niche

Knowledge-based associations are dedicated to achieving outcomes meaningful to those they serve. They focus on the future as much as on the moment; and their activities are tempered by realistic considerations of what they are best able to do. The visions they articulate for their associations describe how the worlds of their members will be different in a better way. Their missions distinguish these organizations from others and reflect their core purposes and ideologies. Their strategies are designed to take full advantage of their tangible and intangible assets, with necessary consideration of other factors in the external environment that may affect their potential for success.

Table 2. Selecting Substantive Strategy: Earning an Identity of Excellence

Operating Model	Will Require
Operational Excellence	
• Deliver a combination of quality, price, and ease of purchase that no one else in the market can match • Not product or service innovators • Do not cultivate one-to-one relationships with customers • Execute extraordinarily well • Committed to guaranteed value	• Cost efficiencies • Large volume for programs that reduce costs • High-quality customer service • Rapid, responsive fulfillment capabilities
Product (Program) Leadership	
• "Leading edge" programs—programs that "expand existing performance boundaries" • Useful new applications of existing programs	• Being creative; processes supporting inventiveness and invention • Entrepreneurial culture; rewarding risk • Scanning mechanisms to identify potential new programs before they become apparent to others • Program development involves business and management processes supporting program development engineered for speed • Willingness to "leapfrog" their own latest program with something new
Customer (Member) Intimacy	
• Builds bonds/relationships with members • Doesn't deliver what the market wants but what a specific customer wants • Knows their member/customers and the products and services they need • Constantly upgrading what they offer to stay one step ahead of their customers • Cultivates its greatest asset of customer loyalty • Commitment is: "We take care of you and your needs"	• Relationship building and maintenance and relationship management capabilities • Ability to customize programs, products, and services • Focus on those they can serve best • Member databases supporting customization • Culture that embraces deep and lasting relationships and specific, rather than general, responses • Delegation of authority to those closest to the member/customer
Representational Effectiveness	
• Successfully advocating the interests of industry, profession, or interest area • Maintains personalized relationships with powerful decision makers • Positions the interests of the constituency as congruent with public and decision maker interests • Earns recognition as the source of member benefit	• Being recognized as a source of valuable information to decision makers • Anticipating knowledge of evolving issues • Timely knowledge of proposals, positions, opinions, and world views of others

Many associations are finding that clarifying the nature of the relationship they intend to have with their members is an important consideration in defining service niche. Four models for excellence, adapted from models employed by for-profit service organizations, are useful tools for knowledge-based associations. They help generate rational consideration of core competencies required to earn a reputation for excellence that distinguish an association from other places that may also seek to serve its members.

Table 2 summarizes the attributes of an association that has effectively committed to relating to its members in a particular way. It also summarizes the core competencies that such a commitment will require for successful execution.

Three of the models in table 2 relate to the nature of the interaction between the organization and its members. A fourth model focuses on the advocacy function of an association. It could be executed with some of the attributes of any of the three previous models. But, because advocacy is a primary business line for so many associations, it provides a particularly useful profile. It illustrates the core competencies involved in earning a reputation for excellence where representation is the organization's primary mission.

Many knowledge-based organizations are likely to select one of the four models as the "key driver" of its processes, human resource strategies, and culture. They will employ the other descriptions as tools for enhancing the performance of specific functions related to another alternative.

CHAPTER 2

Surfing the Wave

During the next twenty years, successful associations will replace political concern about the internal distribution of power with concern about the association's image and working environment. This environment will be characterized by coherency, flexibility, adaptability, responsiveness, speed, and value.

Managing intellectual assets will be an important part of the knowledge-based organization. This entails dealing with both the content of intellectual assets and the association's culture as it relates to using these assets. Managing information is an obligation association staff and elected leaders share.

New Paradigms of Leadership

A useful working definition of leadership is "influencing the behavior of others." The leader's principal currency for doing this is the information others use to make choices or develop judgments and perceptions that determine their behavior. The first obligation an association leader has, therefore, is to ensure that he or she has access to a continuous stream of information from members that keeps him or her aware of their view of the world and what they consider their needs, expectations, and preferences to be.

This is different from what leaders and leaders' colleagues think members ought to think. Leaders must focus on what, in fact, they do think, even if they are wrong. Members of many associations can be wrong a lot. Because they do not have adequate information about capabilities or strategic strengths and vulnerabilities, many members in many associations really do not understand what they need from their associations. Because they may not spend time considering likely futures, they may not have an adequate sense of the opportunities or challenges their future environments may present. Neither of these information deficiencies, however, tend to prevent members from having strong opinions about what they want.

Leaders must develop a special awareness from their access to information. They must integrate sensitivity to members' views of their world with their own, more informed judgments about what may be looming over the horizon and what the association is well positioned to do.

What Members Expect from Leaders

The knowledge-based association operates on a fundamental set of premises about what the membership expects from its leaders, both elected and staff. There are definite things members now expect, some of which are unique to associations. Members expect their leaders to be able to communicate, through language and behavior, three things.

First: Members expect a clear, common, and positive vision of an achievable future. Each of those words is critical, and this particular content must be communicated in a clear, common, and positive fashion because it has more to do with the essential mission and function of the board than anything else. People will not follow negative leadership for long. They will listen at first but, after a while, the damage to the leader, self-inflicted, will be clearly seen. People will not follow someone who brings them bad news, even if the news is correct. The reason, very simply, is that people do not want to feel bad about anything important to them.

Second: Members expect appreciation for their values, expectations, needs, and anxieties. In an earlier book, (Tecker and Fidler 1993), we observed that when executives and boards reach divorce—termination—it is often because the board, or an important part of that board, begins to perceive that concern for the values, expectations, needs, and anxieties of the members no longer exists. Something else appears to be more important to the executive than what the organization is supposed to be doing for its membership. It does not matter whether this condition truly exists or not; if the group perceives this is the case, it will react accordingly.

Third: Members expect optimism that ability, good plans, and hard work will lead to success. Several associations have embedded this statement in their job descriptions for board members. Other associations are using it as an outline for developing criteria that nominating committees consider to make more rationally based, systematic judgments about who should be recommended for leadership positions, recognizing the difference between popularity and competence.

Additionally, they want leaders who can empower people to deliberate effectively through astute management of the dynamics of group process. In an association, more than almost anywhere else, decisions are made in groups. One of the most frustrating things in the world for association executives is that there is often no individual in the association empowered to make a decision alone. However, even in a knowledge-based association, a good leader must expect to sometimes sacrifice speed for involvement.

The Grand Marshall Syndrome

Failure to create access to members' opinions develops the risk that the leader will suffer from the Grand Marshall syndrome. The Grand Marshall's favorite expression is, "My problem is that I'm a leader and that the dummies won't follow."

The Grand Marshall is very bright and committed, but also very quick. Sometimes, the Grand Marshall has the tendency to get so far ahead that he or she cannot see the people being lead anymore, let alone figure out where they need to go. The Grand Marshall has a mental picture of his or her role. He or she is at the head of a parade with a big baton and a large column of people behind. This metaphor worked very well through the 1970s, the 1980s, and maybe even into the beginning of the 1990s.

In the 1990s, a problem began to occur with this picture of leadership. The Grand Marshall was frequently looking back over his or her shoulder to see if people were still there. Eventually, he or she found themselves looking over their shoulder to try to discover what folks were about to do to him or her. As a result, the Grand Marshall had to create a new image of leadership, one that would serve well in a contemporary association.

Leading from the Middle

In the new picture, leaders do not see themselves at the head of a long column; they see themselves in the middle of a row of people extending out on either side. This is referred to as leading from the middle. They see this row on either side, like what used to be called in hockey or football, "the flying wedge."

In viewing this herringbone-like formation, leaders are able to look to both the left and right. If they see that other key players are not quite up to a desired point, they have a few choices. One is to provide information that creates a stronger feeling of need on the part of the people on either side to move a little more quickly to catch up to those who are ahead. Another is to slow down their own pace until the situation causes others to catch up. A third choice is to question whether those people should be out there at all. It is possible that others in the line understood something that they did not. The leaders realize they have those strategic choices because they see themselves leading from the middle.

Informing Members

A special obligation of leadership in a knowledge-based environment is exchanging information. This has to do with the responsibility elected and staff leadership share to ensure that they provide members a coherent stream of information describing the judgments they are making and the reasons for making them. It is necessary to establish such an information exchange to establish a view for members of the world that is shared between members and leadership.

This is not accomplished by a president's column in the organization's newsletter that says, "Here are the seven items the board considered, and here is the decision made on each item." It is accomplished by a continuous dialogue with members using all available media and methods of communication to share not only the judgments made, but also what has served as the basis for those judgments. Opportunities for communication include what leaders write, the statements they make at meetings they attend, what they choose to ask about in surveys and interviews, and both formal and informal conversations in which they participate that refer to these judgments.

To understand the Grand Marshall syndrome, or at least the vulnerability inherent in it, there is a second, equally important consideration for leaders. This is that their view of the world is going to be distorted. Sometimes, the worst source of information about members' views can be the governing board; the second worst can be the chief staff officer; and the third worst can be committee chairs or senior staff.

By virtue of leaders' roles, they spend time in a stream of information that is deeper, broader, and more frequently refreshed and future-oriented than the stream of information the vast majority of an association's membership experiences. That is why it is so critical for association leaders to be able to make decisions based on both sensitivity to members' needs, as they have expressed them, and the leader's own insight about the foreseeable future and the organization's capacity and strategic position.

When outsider and insider views of the present and the possible future are combined with ethical principles in making a judgment, then leadership is exercising informed intuition. Given the rate at which today's world is moving, it is inevitable that leadership successful into the twenty-first century will be increasingly dependent on using informed intuition as the basis for its judgments.

Associations are Voluntary

Another critical notion is recognizing the voluntary nature of the organization. Here there are two important concepts. The first is the perception of "benefit," and the second is the perception of "perceived value."

It may be that the most important factor here is the relationship between these two. In an association, because it is volunteer-intensive by nature, no one has to do anything he or she does not want to do. That is a very different dynamic than exists in other places where an employee/employer relationship exists. Effective leaders constantly articulate the benefits of involvement in the organization to those whose support is being sought. This focus on benefit must operate at every level of a successful association's thinking.

The vision, goals, and strategic objectives of a long-range strategic plan need to be framed in terms describing how the world of an association's membership, or the constituency that its members are serving, will be different in a better way as a result of what the association does. This is a question of benefits. It is a focus on the service niche of the organization in terms that have value to those served.

The second critical concept relates to "perceived values." It refers to the extent to which the organization's culture is perceived by members and potential members as reflecting a set of beliefs and behaviors with which that individual would be proud to be associated.

Demographics and generational diversity seem to be altering what people consider when making the decision to "volunteer."

Fun is Back in Demand

Fun is coming back to associations! And, it's a serious issue—but, responding to it should be an enjoyable process that produces better results and a more rewarding experience. After more than a decade of the baby boomer demand to "get me in, give what I need so I can use it immediately, and get me out," joy is in demand again.

Baby boomers are aging. With the realization that the resplendent material wealth promised in the 1970s and 1980s will not be achieved by everyone, they are returning to an earlier value of being part of something bigger and more important than themselves.

Many have spent a large part of their lives trying to win a "rat race" only to realize that winning still makes them just a rat. Now, they want more. The boom generation has always demonstrated the ability to deal with a realization that they can't have something by devaluing the unreachable and replacing it with a new definition of success.

In their renewed search for meaning, however, the maturing members of the cornucopia generation face some challenges. First, the usual sources of community that were available to previous generations are not available: neighborhoods are too mobile; for many, church or cultural groups aren't cosmopolitan enough; and hardly anybody stays with the same company for a lifetime.

Second, for boomers, a large part of self image has always been based on what they do for a living. This was the generation for whom "certification" of one sort or another defined the difference between their jobs and their careers and became a major industry. While the value of acquiring material goods has diminished for many, few have abandoned their affection for professionalism.

So, where can this largest cohort of the adult population look to satisfy its recommitment to gregarious but meaningful affiliation with others? The opportunity for associations to become this source of community is enormous—if leaders understand the dynamics at work. Because baby boomers still account for most association members today, their demands are strong, and most associations will want to respond.

Pride in Affiliation

Historically, the decision to select and join an association was made based on the match between the perceptions of (1) one's needs and (2) the benefits offered by a particular organization. If its programs satisfied those needs—meaning that the value matched the price of membership—then the individual joined.

Assuming this, organizations used certain techniques to strengthen membership. If an association wanted to attract new members from a non-traditional population, it would add programs targeted to that group. If an association wanted to get existing members more involved, it would upgrade its programming to better match those members' needs. Or, if the match was basically good, it would reinvigorate promotion of its offerings.

Even though those dynamics are still important, our research has identified another variable driving the decision to belong (Tecker and Fidler 1993). It is the extent to which the association earns a perception of being the kind of organization to which a person would be proud to belong. In other words, the key traits of the association need to be congruent with a set of values and an identity that the individual desires. For boomers, the two decision points are usually applied with equal value. For younger members, who are gradually replacing baby boomers as the prospective membership market, this is often the deciding factor.

This personality of an association is often referred to as the "culture of the organization." It is the fabric of *beliefs* and *assumptions* (the view of the world), *values* (what is considered most important in that world view), and typical *behaviors* within the organization. Together, these attributes create what the experience of being involved will be like. Culture differs from association to association—and often among member segments within a single association. Because the pre-boom, boom, and post-boom generations now all want "enjoyable experiences" as much as they want useful content, however, every association will need to attend to the quality of culture as much as it attends to the match between member needs and programs.

There is no single "perfect" culture to act as a panacea for all associations. However, certain characteristics do prevail as being successful. One is a climate that values enjoyable interactions within the association as much as it values hard work and results. It is not suggested that a big banquet with an open bar and humorous speaker will be sufficient. While more and more associations are using "edutainment" technologies to bring more memorable experiences to well-designed meetings, merely incorporating these activities is too simplistic. Associations need to recognize that even the "hard work" of the association needs to be fun.

Hard Work Should Be Fun

Even though some things like working on a committee or serving on a board are hard work, they should still be enjoyable. The time spent with well-intentioned and thoughtful people while working on real issues affecting the industry, profession, or cause must be sufficient to compensate for the dedication involved. For example, a board that has a reputation for spending large amounts of time on administrative tasks will increasingly deter members from wanting to get involved. The board's set of values will be a sufficient obstacle to belonging, even for those who see a good match between their needs and the association's programs.

In fact, our observations suggest that an increasing number of members remember the experience of participating in an event more than they recall the content or results. However, for today's sophisticated consumer of association affiliation this is not an either/or proposition; the demand is for both in an attractive balance.

Associations that fail to take both expectations into consideration risk losing the brightest and most influential members of their industry or profession. Later, this text examines in some detail the likely differences in culture between the traditional or historic culture of twentieth century associations and the attributes of success the next decade will require. One requirement that stands out among many will be this need to define and sustain a culture integrating fun into transactions with current and potential members.

Voluntary associations will need to address this prerequisite for success by consciously integrating culture considerations into strategic thinking about the enterprise. In the knowledge-based association, issues of culture are carefully explored along with decisions about service niche, program, finances, organizational structures, and key processes.

Ride the Crest of the Wave

If you are familiar with the expression, "getting ahead of the curve," we suggest you abandon it! There are two sources to this the expression. One is from sports. Anyone who has played baseball knows that when the pitcher throws a curve ball, you hit the curve ball by hitting it before it breaks—you get "ahead of the curve." Statisticians adopted this expression and applied it to business cycles with the idea that before the success curve heads down, something new should be started to drive the curve up.

"Surfing" is the alternative metaphor suggested here. Here is why. If you have ever surfed waves, you know that the goal is to keep most of the surf board on the crest of the wave, not in front of it. The tip of the board should stick out in front of the wave, but most of the board needs to be right on the breaking crest. If you stay behind the crest you lose momentum and sink. If the whole board gets out in front of the wave, you get swamped.

In a world changing as quickly as it is, most associations are likely to find "surfing" the more fitting metaphor. Get the tip of your board out in front of the wave, but keep most of your weight right on the crest. Not behind it—you will get nowhere. Keep right on the crest!

A good example is the recent experience of one large association that invested several million dollars in studies and design and development work for an information infrastructure that would create user owned and operated access to a database essential to the membership's business operations. The concept was right. Industry ownership of an essential business tool was in the best interest of the membership. A separate board composed of users without sufficient technical expertise, however, approved a network strategy that was outdated even before it was implemented.

Politically charged concern about public access to what had historically been a proprietary database produced a politically correct but technologically naive series of decisions that ignored emerging realities of the marketplace. Products that were superior in utility and cost were launched by some of the organization's own affiliates and members at the same time the organization began to execute its sales plan! Millions of dollars were wasted, and the organization's reputation as an effective industry leader was severely damaged.

Warnings from credible sources were ignored while the organization continued to work hard to "get ahead of the curve" that had already been replaced. Lack of expertise, imposing the political model of decision making historically employed by the association on its new business model, and the natural slowness of a culture overly concerned about power distribution combined to create a disaster that would have been avoided by a more knowledge-based operation.

Instead of talking about getting out in front of the wave, association leaders should think in terms of surfing the wave, specifically what they ought to be doing to provide oversight that is guided by foresight. Certainly it is necessary to look at context and think about important questions that affect the current world of members, but it is also vital to know what you must do as a leader to get the organization to take constructive action while anticipating the possibility of significant change. In today's climate of rapid and complex change, leadership's primary responsibility is to ensure the proper questions are continually asked and answered. If the leadership has questions about what the organization should be doing, the simplest, best solution is to make sure that the right questions get discussed and answered by people with sufficient and appropriate knowledge.

By whom and where should questions of strategic direction be resolved? These conversations, which should be ongoing, must occur at meetings of the governing board. That group has the responsibility, legitimacy, and credentials to continuously attend to issues related to strategic direction. That does not mean that you, the leader, cannot get other groups together to think about things in different ways. In fact, knowledge-based governance considers what it does not know as carefully as it builds on what it does understand. Leadership of organizations "surfing the wave" expect that other groups will be increasingly needed to serve as sources of insight, ideas, and information to their governing boards.

If the governing board is not actively engaged in considering strategic direction issues, decisions about policy, programming, and budget are likely to be made by the board with little reference or relevance to the truly significant and often emerging strategic issues confronting the organization. Priorities are set in the budgeting process based on politics, perceptions, and past practice with insufficient consideration of future implications.

Avoiding the "Roberts' Rules" Restraint

Behavior at board meetings is becoming decidedly more corporate and much less political in associations moving toward a knowledge-based operational philosophy. Moreover, there appears to be a growing abandonment of Robert's Rules, except for the portion of the rules that have to do with making, seconding, and voting on motions.

When associations merely employ Robert's Rules of Order and conduct a formal meeting, "conversations" do not happen. Robert's Rules of Order are meant to be a tool for: (1) satisfying corporate law; (2) maintaining corporate civility in emotional or political discussions; (3) assuring that all participants are afforded an equal and democratic chance to be heard; and (4) maintaining order in the flow of business. They were never meant to be a restraint.

There are two things to do if their use inhibits open discussion. One is to convene a conference, meeting, seminar, or retreat where you are not engaged in the business of the organization. Have tables set up differently, tell people to dress differently, and hold it in a different environment. Give people every signal you can that this is an opportunity for strategic thinking, but do not convene the gathering as a business meeting. Under such circumstances it is remarkably easy to be open, honest, and stretch the envelope. In exchange for that comfort, let participants know that they are not to be making any decisions that day.

The second possibility, if it is necessary to cause a change in behavior during the meeting itself, is to use Robert's Rules of Order to move to "a committee of the whole." When a group moves to a committee of the whole, it is essentially suspending Robert's Rules of Order. You do not need motions or seconds; all that formality is off. Anyone can talk, so long as the chair recognizes him or her. But there is a trade off: while in a committee of the whole, no decisions are permitted; no resolutions may be entertained.

Moving to a committee of the whole signals to the board that it is about to abandon the normal fashion of discussion and decision making, with no resolutions allowed or decisions made, to encourage open, constructive conversation. This is done to learn things, to think through something so the group with responsibility for execution has the benefit of the entire group's thinking. It also alerts the group to other issues it might have to deal with later as part of the business meeting.

Finally, a motion to adjourn from a committee of the whole and move back into the formal meeting, the only motion that is allowed, may be entertained. This technique, in effect, creates walls around those portions of the meeting, facilitates open discussion, and helps greatly to maintain order in the formal part of the meeting.

Conversely, occasionally there is a nefarious use of the technicalities of parliamentary procedure, indicating that a group of somewhat less than honest people is trying to move an issue in a particular direction by manipulating the rules rather than dealing with the substance of the issue. This occurs in the U.S. Congress, and it is a movement directly away from commitment to a knowledge-based culture. Using Roberts' Rules this way usually means that the group has decided it is and will be perceived as wrong and will be outvoted, so it tries to use the rules as an obstruction strategy.

CHAPTER 3

Building Industry Foresight—Developing Vision, Mission, Goals

Lewis Carroll in his classic, *Alice in the Looking Glass*, introduces a character called the Cheshire Cat. This rolly poly, reclined, feline-like creature is notorious for saying something, smiling, and then disappearing. At one point in her journey through Wonderland, Alice meets the Cheshire Cat at a fork in the road and asks which path she should take. The Cheshire Cat asks where it is she wants to go.

Where do successful associations look for the answer to the Cheshire Cat's question? They tend to look in two places: Outside themselves and into tomorrow. That constitutes developing industry foresight.

Associations successful in sustaining effective positions tend to look outward for opportunities. These associations seek other models, ideas, best practices, and benchmarks from a variety of organizations from both the not-for-profit and the private sectors. They go outside the world view of their leadership to embrace constituencies on their fringes, such as younger and ethnic- and gender-diverse members with different points of view.

They commit to being responsive rather than reactive—and there is a difference. A reactive association tries to do something about a problem after it has passed through the fan. A responsive association tries to anticipate what may be headed for the fan even before members are aware that something is flying.

Leaders do have some choices. They can move the fan, try to deflect what is coming around it, or at least give good advice on how to clean up after what hit the fan has been distributed.

All such alternatives, however, require associations to look outside themselves, as opposed to inside. Basically, the leader must lead the organization and its members where they want to go, even though they may not know they want to go there yet. By doing this, not only does the organization sustain effective position but, by creating its future, it does not simply satisfy its members, it often amazes them.

Answering Four Key Questions

An organization with a knowledge-based operational philosophy creates an environment of awareness of what is coming. This allows an association to participate in shaping its world rather than becoming a victim of a world shaped by others. Four key questions must be answered to create this environment.

Question 1.

What assumptions can be made about the future environment of the industry, profession, constituency group, or issue arena?

Assumptions are subtly, but significantly, different than trends. A trend is a change in progress and direction. Trends are something you see happening at the moment that can be used as the basis for a judgment about where things are going to go.

Assumptions do not require you to be able to identify anything happening at the moment to project something that might happen in the future. An assumption could just as well come from informed intuition. Again, informed intuition is the sense you get when your right brain interacts with your left brain and you think, "I can't really put my finger on what's going to make this happen, but my experience, my instinct, and the time I'm spending in the stream of information suggests that it's feasible that, at some point, this could be." That is an assumption.

How are Assumptions Used?

Here are some examples of assumptions made by other organizations thinking strategically about the future. They are examples of format, not necessarily content. One group, in looking at external environment and resources, assumed changes in technology would have a major impact on services and would increasingly affect all aspects of services. That is an example of an assumption.

Another group, looking at consumers, assumed clients and consumers would be increasingly involved and would be much more knowledgeable and demanding about their choices and rights and that they would seek better values with no price increases. That was an assumption they made about the future, grounded in trends.

Here is a unique example related to the structure of service delivery. A group assumed that the structure of service delivery, while difficult to predict, would likely be different from what is in place today. There may be consolidations, takeovers by larger organizations, and more alliances. Some of those alliances might be with former competitors or current suppliers.

This example of an assumption is unique because the group didn't have the foggiest idea of what the future would really be like. That assumption is pretty important for an association because it has extraordinary implications for its macro strategy.

If you are an association leader and you assume that you do not really know how things are going to turn out, you have developed some information about the direction the organization's general strategy should take. For example, from this assumption, you may decide only to commit to initiatives that are not so long term. Now, there might be a longer-term vision, but you are not going to commit to something unless it can be easily altered or abandoned. You are not going to get into a contract that you cannot change in favor of something else that is more important if a new reality emerges. You still have the big picture of what the end might look like, but you need flexibility.

It also means that any significant initiative you engage in needs to be one that is carefully benchmarked at the front end. You want to be able to tell quickly whether initiatives are still responsive to the environment as the environment changes.

Such judgments and approaches operate at all levels and in all places in a knowledge-based organization. *When you use informed intuition, you start out by viewing the world and admitting that you do not really know how all things will turn out.*

Knowledge-based organizations seek to remain as agile as possible. If such is the nature of your environment, if assumptions about the future are critical for you, then your key strategic imperative is to remain nimble. You must be able to shift if you need to—externally in what you deliver, and internally in how you operate the organization. This is sometimes uncomfortable for organizations that have developed large, entrenched political bureaucracies, often reflected in numerous standing committees.

Articulating Vision is Critical

When an organization does not understand the future it frequently does nothing. That could be worse than doing something, even if what is done is wrong. That is especially apt to be true for an association because the consequence of doing nothing is that membership, looking for something, migrates elsewhere. By the time it has figured out something it is comfortable doing, it has lost the critical mass needed to do anything well.

That's why clarity and commitment to what will constitute success is so important. If an organization is able to define its vision and goals in ways that describe the way it would like the world to be, it can make judgments about what it will or will not do within that changing context, even when it does not know exactly what to do. When associations make assumptions about the future, the specific solutions required, should those assumptions come to pass, may not always be known. By thinking about the future in this manner, however, associations are better able to fashion them.

There is a psychological aspect to leadership's use of vision in a knowledge-based organization during troubled times. It helps when people can agree that they are better off staying in the boat until they get to a point where it is clear that the boat has to be abandoned and the "every man for himself" approach is necessary. The more turbulent the water, the more important it is to articulate a vision of what it is going to feel like when you finally get to shore.

Question 2.

What one or two innovations or occurrences, which are not possible today, could happen that would fundamentally change your industry or profession?

This involves thinking about the unthinkable. A real example occurred ten years ago with a premier medical specialty society. They were thinking about the future for the purpose of crafting a longer-range strategy.

The group was asked what they would do if somebody came along and decided that their medical specialty made too much money, that a cap should be put on the fees they could charge for certain procedures, and that the remaining dollars should be redistributed to other specialties that focused on preventive medicine. The response of the group a decade ago was, "This could never happen." "What group could possibly possess the power to make this occur?" And finally, "It's not American." This example more that adequately demonstrates the value of being willing to stretch the envelope and think about the inconceivable.

Question 3.

Where do those you serve, your members and the industry or profession, want to go, that they don't know about yet?

The answers to questions one and two provide a platform of information you can use to answer this. Here is the linkage. The first question asked what the condition of the world would be like in the future. The second question asked whether anything might come along that could significantly alter that condition and, if it did, what that condition would be. Now, the question is, "If this is what the condition of the world is going to be in the future, what needs or opportunities will be presented for your members that they might not even be thinking about yet because they have not even thought that the world might look like this?"

Question 4.

If such will be the condition of the world you expect in the foreseeable future, and here is the need or opportunity that condition might create for your members, then what should you, as an association leader, consider doing to respond?

This final question builds off the previous one and begins to create internal focus on what opportunities have not been seen, articulated, or exploited by others. You "surf the wave" thinking this way.

A knowledge-based organization is better able to migrate uncomfortable dilemmas because it considers the future and how to respond to it before it becomes a present-day crisis. Organizations cannot slow down or stop a marketplace dynamic that is in the best interest of consumers. To try to do so is foolish. It devours a tremendous amount of resources and energy and causes lost opportunities. All this energy could, instead, be directed to giving real assistance members need to deal with tomorrow's dilemmas.

There is always a group in an organization that says, "Please, stop this," and another group that says, "I know those changes are coming; I know we have to do this, but could you just leave it alone for another five years until I'm out of here?" These individuals all fear dealing with change and breaking out of the organization's patterns of the past. They may also be among the association's most core members. Organizations can choose to acquiesce to these concerns, but still unknown will be whether those segments of members will still be in business five years later facing the same dynamics in their industries that they never wanted to address.

A Clear Service Niche

Knowledge-based associations are clear on their "service niche." A service niche is like a market niche, but a little different. In the knowledge-based association, a service niche involves essential needs of its members that no other organization is as well positioned to meet.

The phrase, "essential needs" is key. Not basic, or sophisticated—we are speaking here of *essential* needs that must be met. Not could be met, would be nice to meet, but *must* be met. These needs are of a nature that no other organization, private vendor, association, academic institution, or government, is as well positioned to meet them. An organization's ability to focus on a service niche and match it to its core capabilities is an indispensable ingredient to its future success.

Thinking about the future is critical. Having discussions about what could be, ought to be, and should be, are important to surf the wave, to be responsive. There will always be a number of individuals in an organization who, in the course of the retreat, the planning conference, or board discussion on such items, will say, with complete legitimacy, "This stuff is all well and good, but when are we going to decide what we are going to do this year?"

Therefore, when you engage in discussions about tomorrow, reserve time to turn the organization's attention to a more short-range time frame. Ask and answer this question, as well, "In the next two years, considering the necessity of achieving a few significant wins, if our organization is to be recognized as remaining viable, what are the strategic issues we must address?" This links your more abstract thinking about the outside environment and the future with more practical decisions you are making about the priorities for work in the coming year or two.

When this question is asked and answered on the heels of the discussion about the future you just had, the answers you get are very different than if you had just opened the floor to suggestions about what you need to do next. Absent the longer-term view first, you tend to get a long list of good ideas and end up committing to an idea that was (1) thought of first, (2) articulated by the most eloquent or powerful individual, or (3) being supported by the person who talked the longest and loudest. You went along with it just to quiet him or her; but it may not have been the most strategically correct idea.

When you address this issue of current activity within the larger context of future activity, the perspective is very different.

Answering the Cheshire Cat

Remember our earlier reference to *Alice Through the Looking Glass or Alice in Wonderland*? There is more to the episode where Alice gets to a fork in the road and meets the Cheshire Cat.

Alice gets to the fork in the road, encounters the Cheshire Cat, and asks, "Which of these paths should I take?" The Cheshire Cat says, "Easy question, easy answer. Where do you want to go?" Alice replies, "Well, I really don't know where I want to go." The Cheshire Cat instantly responds, "Still an easy answer, either path will do!"

A major responsibility shared by staff and elected leadership is to ensure that, at any point in time, your organization has a satisfactory answer for the Cheshire Cat. Note the language here. The obligation is to ensure that the organization has a satisfactory answer; it is not your job to personally or benevolently declare what that answer should be.

One very experienced association executive once made the observation that she used to take a great deal of pride in making a good decision, and she does not anymore. Now, as a highly experienced executive of an association, she takes pride in ensuring that a good decision is made. This evolved perception of personal reward is an important attribute of leadership in a knowledge-based enterprise.

That is something your organization depends on you to do. However, at the very moment you are executing that very special responsibility you have as a leader, that of thinking about the future, you are also most vulnerable to the Grand Marshall syndrome. There is no topic about which it is more tempting to express your own opinion than the future.

In fact, at the very moment you are doing what leaders, especially, must do, that is—think about tomorrow—it becomes most important for you to ensure that you have access to all the information bases that informed intuition demands. By using informed intuition in an environment operating with a knowledge-based philosophy, leaders can influence the behavior of others in ways most likely to produce preferred futures for their organizations.

Here is how that works. Imagine that you have been fairly successful in identifying your members' needs. That is, you have been fairly successful in identifying the highest-priority needs of your most significant membership segments of the moment—an important set of qualifiers for a world of rapid change. You have dipped the bucket in a moving information stream, looked in a series of buckets, and you are pretty confident you know what people want something done about. On the basis of those judgments you are prepared to set some direction.

Vision, Mission, Goals

In an association, a good vision usually has two parts. Part one is its external dimension; part two, its internal. The external dimension of the vision describes how the world of the member will be different in a better way as a result of, at least in part, whatever it is the association does. This dimension of vision does not describe at all what the association should be like or what it intends to do. It describes the way it would like the world to be if it could influence it to become that way.

The internal dimension of vision is more traditional. It is the part that identifies what the key traits of the organization ought to be and that describes its personality, its character.

The external dimension articulates the way the organization would like to get the world to reshape itself. The internal dimension articulates the kind of entity the organization needs to be to have the best chance of influencing the world and moving in the desired direction.

From vision can be extracted mission, which declares the fundamental purpose for which the organization exists. If vision describes the way the organization would like the world to be, mission articulates what specific role the organization intends to play in pursuing that vision. It does this while recognizing that there may be other groups either contributing to that pursuit or inhibiting it, some of which the organization may not be able to control at all.

From vision, goals are also extrapolated. Goals are more specific statements that represent commitments made to the membership. A goal describes a condition or attribute the organization is trying to reach. It does not talk about strategy, what will be done, how it will be done, or who will do it. It just talks about what the organization is trying to accomplish.

Suppose, for example, you are leading a vocational society, and one of the things that is very important to your membership is that they be satisfactorily recognized by those who employ them. If they are contractors, they want to be recognized by their clients; if they are staff members, they want to be recognized by their employers. A goal statement might say, "Members of the ABC vocation will be recognized and appreciated by their clients or employers, and the value of their contribution will be understood and appropriately compensated." That is what is meant by a goal.

Goals do not discuss what the organization is going to do to get there. The organization is still articulating where it is trying to go. That is part of its answer to the Cheshire Cat.

Here is another example: Suppose you are leading a trade association, and one of the things that is very important to your members, in an industry where the business structure is changing through aggregation and consolidation, is the trend of niching to either very large or very small (very large competing on the basis of cost, very small competing on the basis of differentiation). Although this creates multiple membership marketplaces (member segments with different needs that you are trying to serve), what they all share in common is the need for access to certain kinds of information. They all need operational information, benchmarking information, and marketing information that lets them make more effective business decisions within these circumstances.

A goal statement, in this case, might say something like, "Members of the XYZ association will have instant access to the information and insight they require to effectively make successful business decisions in today's business climate." Again, note that you have not said anything yet about what or how.

What you have said is, "Here is the outcome we are shooting for. Here is the benefit. Here is our answer to the Cheshire Cat."

Developing Strategy

From its vision, mission, and goals, associations are able to articulate strategy. Strategy answers the question: What kinds of things is the organization going to do to move toward achieving the outcomes declared important?

It is very hard to have confidence in decisions about the kind of work needed if no understanding has been reached about what the organization is trying to accomplish. It is very unlikely that people will ever be able to agree on how to get somewhere if they have not first agreed on where they are going.

Once this direction is established, and assuming the leadership has previously reached consensus and clarity on what constitutes success, the association is in a position to decide about the kind of work it needs to do. In an association, work is usually organized into programs and services. Decisions must be made about the business lines in which the organization will be involved, what programs or services will be offered within those business lines, and what events and activities will be parts of those programs and services.

Once an organization has decided on the work required, it can discuss implementation. This involves how it can best organize to get this work done and what kind of operating and support systems should be used to efficiently carry it out.

In an organization with a knowledge-based operational philosophy, when leadership has done a good job, the results are meaningful benefits to its members, prospective members, customers, and the communities they serve.

Differences Between Effectiveness and Efficiency

Association leaders often engage in decision making about effectiveness and efficiency. They are not the same thing. "Effectiveness" answers the question, "Am I doing the right thing?" "Efficiency" answers the question, "Am I doing things right?"

In a knowledge-based association, leadership's special responsibility is to focus on effectiveness issues to ensure that the organization is doing the right thing. Unfortunately, many organizations are highly efficient and not at all effective. They are often moving with all deliberate speed to all the wrong places and getting there much more quickly than they ever thought possible. It is not a case of being one or the other; an association needs to be effective and efficient. The special obligation of leadership is to ensure that the boat is being steered in the right direction so those who are rowing know where to put the pressure.

In a knowledge-based organization, how much is leadership involved in efficiency and how much in effectiveness? The answer depends on the size of the organization, the leadership structure, the number of individuals or groups available to get work done, and the ways the work gets done. The smaller the association, the more likely leadership is involved in both. The larger the association, the more complex is its program of work. The more sophisticated is its strategy, the less likely that leadership is involved in both efficiency and effectiveness. The most successful associations have been those where the culture exhibits sufficient trust to permit leadership to focus its attention on effectiveness. They use other expert, less preoccupied sources to focus on issues of efficiency and getting things done right.

Generally, on an effective board's agenda, 70 percent or more agenda items should be directly related to issues of strategic direction or policy. If the percentage is less, then the board is probably engaged in what might be called "administrivia." Administrivia involves focusing on operational issues rather than strategic intent and desired outcomes. Administrivia often leads to "snoopervision." Snoopervision occurs when the absence of clarity about desired outcomes leaves supervisors with no alternative to exercising oversight, other than meddling with the details of how objectives will be achieved.

There are two problems here. One is, if the board is engaged in administrivia, who is making decisions about where the association is going to go? One answer is "no one,"—where the group is going is an accident dependent on what happens over time. The other problem is, if leadership is spending its time on the how-to's, talking about what color the brochure should be, and where the meeting site should be, rather than talking about whether to have an annual meeting at all, then who is talking about what the group must accomplish? The answer here, again, is no one; or, sometimes, senior staff is drawn to fill the vacuum.

That causes real problems because it starts a clock ticking; you can hear toe tapping until, inevitably, somebody says, "Hey, whose place is this, anyhow?" For the staff executive forced into considering effectiveness issues because his or her board spent all its time thinking about efficiency, the unintended consequence of this reversal of roles is conflict that leads to a job search.

Setting Priorities

If the existing condition suggests greater demand and opportunity than capacity, setting priorities becomes critical. Suppose leadership has a list of a hundred good ideas. What strategy can a leader use to get that list whittled down and focused on the most critical, essential things to do? How, with a knowledge-based, operational philosophy, are priorities identified?

A rule for successful association leaders in a knowledge-based environment is that member needs should be satisfied first. Once member needs have been considered, appropriate long-term program and organizational strategy should be developed to respond to the anticipated future environment. If leadership does not first set priorities among needs and opportunities, they are inviting strident emotion and heavy politics from the dialogue that will ensue about which programs ought to get attention, because every program has a constituency.

There are four criteria that have proved useful in helping sort priorities. Again, leadership has a list of a hundred good ideas. Realizing the need for incremental wins, the two or three most important things must be narrowed down from that list.

Criterion 1. Impact—The first thing to do is to look at each item on the list and assess it in terms of "impact." Impact is a measure of strategic importance relevant to the relationships among things. It is likely that some of the items on that list are related to several other items. The greater the number of other items related to an item, the higher is its strategic importance, the higher is its impact.

Criterion 2. Consequence—Second, "consequence" is a measure of strategic importance that has to do with things on that list that, if you do something about them, produce great results. There are other items on that list which, if you do not do anything about them, result in disasters. The greater the significance of either effectively addressing or not addressing the issue, the greater the intensity of the consequence and the higher the strategic importance.

Criterion 3. Immediacy—The third criterion is "immediacy," which is a measure of strategic importance that has to do with time. It has two dimensions. One has to do with sequence. Some of the items on that list of one hundred need to be done before others can be done. The earlier the item appears in the sequence, the higher the immediacy. The higher the immediacy, the higher the strategic importance.

The second dimension has to do with the "window of opportunity." Some things on the list of one hundred ideas will have a larger opening of the window than others. The smaller the opening of the window, the higher the immediacy because there is less time to do something with the issue before either it wrecks the association or the opportunity disappears. Again, the higher the immediacy, the higher the strategic importance.

No one criterion is more important than any other. They can be used together as a general framework to create a rational basis for and consistency in determining the most important thing to do.

Criterion 4. Likelihood of Success—Assume that, out of the list of a hundred, leadership get down to ten or fifteen ideas, based on these criteria. One more criterion will apply, and this one must be applied to the surviving subset of ten or fifteen. This criterion is "likelihood of success." Look at the ten or fifteen good ideas that have survived the previous tests, and ask how likely it is that the organization will be able to implement them in some successful, meaningful way. Does the association have the capacity and strategic position necessary to be successful here? If the answer to this is "no," take it off the list. If the answer is "yes," that helps focus on the two or three that are most important to do in a short time frame.

A Few Wins are Important

It is very important to look at likelihood of success because leadership is looking for "a few significant wins." It is desirable to "stretch" the organization, but the last thing to do is to build a list of good ideas the association does not have the slightest chance of implementing. Leadership generally tries to engender an image of vitality in most associations by demonstrating that people can make a difference, so it is critical to commit to priorities that can be implemented successfully. Leadership does not want to make commitments to a series of high, unachievable priorities. What would that say to members or prospective members about the organization?

In associations that are not knowledge based in their approaches, a frequent error is failure to adequately consider issues of capacity, core capability, and strategic position in deciding what to do. Leadership should not raise expectations to a point they cannot deliver. If that becomes a pattern, both current and prospective members migrate to other places with a better track record.

No matter how politically or emotionally attractive a commitment might be, an association needs to evaluate its chance of success. That does not mean abandoning commitments to things an association may not be able to do successfully. It means wise association leaders take the time to build capacity and strategic position while they amass a record of wins on things that make more immediate differences.

Governing boards must consider these kinds of things. Elected and staff leadership should be facilitating, catalyzing, and encouraging dialog on these issues. These concepts exemplify ways of thinking that reflect commitment to being a knowledge-based association.

CHAPTER 4

Building Effective Board Partnerships

Look, even quickly, at the nature of the partnership between the chief staff officer and the chief elected officer in an association. The degree to which that partnership is functional, that there is communication, and that there is trust and a sense that relationships complement each other, will give you a pretty good idea of what kind of year that association is going to have.

Use Time Well

Associations should examine how their boards spend time together. Good boards spend their time using information, not collecting it. Good boards have information relating to decisions collected before the discussion. An association moving toward becoming knowledge based makes a wealth of relevant information available to its board before a meeting so the board has time to reflect. This increases the degree of comfort members have in speaking, contributing, or committing once the group is assembled.

When a knowledge-based board is in session, it is not the board's role to take in information; it is the board's role to develop insight and to make decisions on information it has already received. Ninety percent of the time at a board meeting should not be consumed with reports; instead 80 percent of the time should be taken up with dialogue, deliberation, and decision making.

Three Major Roles of Boards

In a knowledge-based association, boards typically understand and balance three roles. In their corporate role, they hire and, sometimes, relieve the chief staff officer. They oversee implementation of the strategic plan and oversee the association's portfolio of products, programs, and services.

In their legislative role they establish internal policy which, in its most simplistic sense, is the distribution of responsibility. Usually, bylaws lodge all initial power in the board, and then the board may state, via policy, how it will delegate some of this power. For example, the board may delegate some power to standing committees and some to the executive committee.

A second part of the legislative role is developing external policy. Here a board takes positions on external issues important to members. These are public policy issues on which taking a position is desirable.

Finally, a board must often assume the role of judge when asked to make, take, or choose a position between some competing or conflicting entities within the association.

Board Functions

The governing body for most associations, boards behave many different ways. Some boards accept and exercise the responsibilities they should. Others function more as rubber-stamping entities, not because their executive committees set out to usurp their power, but because these boards were not addressing the tough issues, creating a power vacuum.

Boards have many functions. They approve outcomes to be accomplished, monitor outcomes, determine what they want to have happen, and establish direction. They stay out of process, supervision, and the details of operations.

They provide focus for the organization. This represents the impact and responsibility the board holds as a leadership team to help target the thinking of the organization and its working groups on the right things.

Once outcomes are determined, the board must ensure that the entities expected to carry them out (committees, staff, whoever it happens to be) are allocated the rights and resources to make them happen. They should be able to monitor and ensure that work groups are achieving the desired outcomes.

The Culture of a Knowledge-Based Board

One of the most important underpinnings of the successful association executive in a knowledge-based environment is his or her efforts and ability to orient and work with the board. Board members can become either partners or piranhas which, in great part, is up to the executive.

Orientation

There is a special, nontraditional type of agenda for a board orientation meeting. The first thing done in a meeting with this special agenda is to engage in an activity with the board that directs its attention to the kinds of things boards ought to do. This allows the executive to establish parity in his or her relationship with board members and gives him or her and board members an opportunity to learn a great deal more about what each feels is important, what their values are, and the kinds of experience each brings to their position.

The reason this type of agenda is valuable is because association board members have a tendency to want their association to run the way their business is supposed to run. ("Is supposed to run," is not necessarily the way, in reality, it may actually run. This will be explored in detail as the relationships are examined.)

Certified public accountants have a tendency to pay attention to certain parts of a report when it is presented at board meetings—and can you guess which reports they have a tendency to pay attention to? Dentists have a tendency to want their association executive to run the office like they were told their dental practices were supposed to run.

In associations of engineers or physicists there exists great attention to detail and an assumption that the world will work in the very logical, linear, cause-and-effect fashion that these board members bring with them to the decision process. Unfortunately, however, that is not always the way human behavior works.

There exists a long-standing discussion about the fundamental differences between the boards of private-sector business enterprises and the boards of associations. An association's mission and its measures of success are fundamentally different from those of proprietary, private organizations. The role of the for-profit board is to make sure that the organization "finds some holes and is the place that fills them," hopefully, at a price that exceeds the cost of filling the whole so a profit is generated. The role of the not-for-profit board is to make sure that the organization finds holes that need to be filled, and then to ensure that someone fills them.

If the hole can be better filled by another provider, the strategic association will find a way to create access to that superior response for its members. While an association will not be run exactly like a business, this is not to say that it cannot be run in a businesslike fashion.

Consensus and the Leadership Partnership

Some people have come to believe that consensus occurs in a group when everyone agrees totally. Realistically, in most associations, if you put five board members in a room, there will probably be nine opinions.

A different interpretation of "consensus" is suggested here. It is extraordinarily useful in knowledge-based associations because collaboration and cooperation are the fundamental driving forces in getting things done. Consensus occurs when no one in the group disagrees so strongly with what has been suggested that he or she will not go along with it for the time being.

If you think about it, that is really how groups make progress. In a knowledge-based approach, however, there is a caveat. Leadership must be particularly sensitive to ensuring that it is not always the same person or small group of people that have to go along with what has been proposed. When that happens over time, you get what we call the "French Revolution Syndrome." If you are ever in a meeting where someone on the board is sitting at the back of the room knitting names into a scarf, it is probably a good time to ask for a recess.

Although trade and professional associations do have some significant differences, they are fundamentally similar in the nature of the mission and functions of the board and executive in a knowledge-based organization. When there exists an understanding of what it is boards and executives are to be doing together, it is evident that both good and bad directly result from those common responsibilities. This is what is referred to as the "leadership partnership."

It is crucial for boards to understand their roles and purposes, their needs, and the needs of staff. Many association executives have these insights but, unfortunately, not all boards do. This is critical because if the executive does not provide the opportunity for the board to do the right things, the board will find other things to do. In a knowledge-based system, the decision process is structured as a partnership. This is not to establish the content of deliberation, but to provide a focus for deliberating on those things a board ought to be doing because nobody else can do them.

When leadership in a knowledge-based association has ensured that a board's deliberation is truly information based, it can take satisfaction not in making the decision, but in seeing that a good decision has been made. If you concentrate on getting your board to address issues and problems in a collaborative, systematic fashion based on accurate and timely information, you have every right to expect an effective leadership partnership. Your board members will be partners, not piranhas.

Elements of Effective Leadership Partnerships

We do know some things about effective partnerships in knowledge-based cultures. Both executive and elected leadership must represent the association with an articulate, positive, and practical but dignified presence. Both must fulfill the functions and responsibilities of their particular offices.

In an effective partnership there are common expectations. Again, there is very little chance that people will be able to agree on how to get somewhere, if they have not first agreed on where it is they are going.

We once had an opportunity to watch a municipal body spend forty-five minutes arguing about how the lines on a new football field should be drawn, until somebody discovered that half of the board thought they were talking about a football field and the other half thought they were talking about a soccer field. The more basic the question, the more important it is to make sure that there is a clear, common, and positive vision of it.

Through cooperative planning, common expectations are achieved. Something else also happens in cooperative planning. For the board to do what it is supposed to do, two things must take place. First, it has to understand those common expectations, and, second, it has to be committed to them. If the board does not understand the "hows" and the "whys," then it will not know what to do, and if the board is not committed to them, then it will not bother to see them through.

There is only one way to garner understanding and commitment, and that is through involvement. Cooperative planning builds that kind of shared ownership. Boards need the opportunity to engage in planning at an appropriate level, that is, planning focusing on strategic direction, outcome achievement, and policy.

One of the most difficult aspects of becoming knowledge based is helping the board understand the primary function of this leadership partnership between it and its senior staff. If people do not understand their functions, then they cannot tell whether what they are doing is what they are supposed to be doing. The function of a board and its executives is to pay attention to what is happening overall in the organization.

Good communication and information play very important roles in determining board behavior. Cooperative evaluation of progress—not just summative evaluation, but formative evaluation—is essential in a knowledge-based environment.

Formative Versus Summative Evaluation

Summative evaluation is a system where, at some point in time, the organization looks back and decides whether it achieved what it set out to do and whether it was satisfied with what happened. A performance appraisal system represents a good example of a traditional summative evaluation.

In *formative evaluation* a planning and appraisal system is built in partnership with the knowledge-based board. Here things are examined as they unfold to see whether progress is being made in the desired direction. Problems, progress, and next steps, are all evaluated to determine whether the group is headed where it wants to go. Adjustments can be made if and as necessary.

If you are an airline pilot, summative evaluation of your landing does you very little good. It is not particularly useful to discover after landing that you have missed the runway.

Formative evaluation, however, is very useful to you as a pilot. As you are approaching the runway, it tells you whether you are too high, too low, too far to the left, or too far to the right, and you adjust your course accordingly.

In a knowledge-based system, such a process does two things. First, it builds in an early warning system for the executive, the board, and for the organization. Information is used to make adjustments, not simply to catch somebody doing something wrong and place blame.

Second, formative evaluation also helps leaders focus attention on the things it has declared to be the most critical. With this focus, the board is provided an opportunity to do the right thing. It is not just focusing its attention on (1) things that it may merely be comfortable with or (2) the kinds of things board members think they know about because of the nature of their outside roles.

Neither the aims of the board nor of the executive should be considered superior or inferior. Proper behavior between the board and the executive and between senior staff and the board does not mean that the hierarchy of governance is ignored. Behavior is necessary that facilitates a common understanding of where we are going, why, how we will get there, and how we will know that we are there.

Three Arenas Make Up the Big Picture

There are three kinds of active arenas that, together, constitute the "Big Picture" for an association. One of those arenas is the *arena of mission*. This relates to why the organization exists; what it is going to do; and its mission, goal, objectives, and action plans. It involves strategies as to how it will pursue the fulfillment of its mission. It answers the question of "why."

The second arena has to do with *organization and operations*: how the association is organized and who reports to whom on what kinds of things and how. What are the procedures? How do things get done? What systems are in place? What is the capitalization system, the technical system, and what is the decision-making system? How good is the match between talents and needs? In an association, because it is driven by volunteers, the match between talents and needs is especially important. In large measure, success will depend on the ability to achieve a good match between what people do well and want to do and what the organization needs to have done.

The third arena is *group process*. This concerns the way people behave. It concerns how people navigate in an association which, by definition, gets things done through collaboration and cooperation. This way of getting things done represents a knowledge-based association's power, its competitive edge. While each of these three arenas has been defined separately for the purpose of discussion, they are very much interrelated. If something occurs in one arena it will have a dramatic effect on the others.

For example: If an association's board does not know where it is supposed to be going; if the mission and goals are not clearly articulated, there is very little chance that it will ever be able to organize, establish procedures, implement systems, or match talent to needs in a fashion that will accomplish anything significant.

No matter how clear and articulate an organization's statement of mission is, no matter how well conceived operations are, if people want to pull the rug out from underneath something, they can. In an association where mission is unclear, where there is not a clear, common, and positive vision of an achievable future, people have a tendency to display "turf protection" behavior. Here the board degenerates into a collection of individuals, each with his own personal agenda.

Boards have a function—and there is a difference between a function and a task. A task is something you do, and it is done; a function is how you go about doing what you are supposed to be doing. The board's function, and responsibility, in collaboration with senior staff (that leadership partnership), is to continually monitor the effectiveness of what is occurring in each of these arenas and to monitor the quality of the interaction among the three. This constitutes the "Big Picture."

Perception is Reality

One of the primary roles of leadership in a knowledge-based enterprise is to assist in providing continuous coherence and consistency. With this understanding of function, let us look at why boards behave as they do and what things can be done in a knowledge-based system to influence that behavior.

There are reasons why a board behaves the way it does. Several rules seem to explain its behavior.

Rule No. 1: *What is perceived, is*. That means that if Pat believes that there were little people chasing Pat with ray guns, Pat will behave as though there are little people chasing Pat with ray guns. It does not matter whether they are really there or not. If Pat thinks they are there, then Pat will behave accordingly. Board leaders behave in particular ways and come to certain judgments because they hold opinions based on perceptions they have.

Rule No. 2: *Perceptions are based on available information*. The word "available" does not necessarily mean "true," "complete," or "timely." "Available" means "available." One primary source of available information is past experience. Another primary source is individuals who have certain kinds of information.

Often, in a traditional association that is not knowledge based, boards or board leaders behave certain ways, reaching judgments and holding opinions based on perceptions they have that may be founded on incomplete, inaccurate, out-of-date, or untimely information. These reasons do not matter to them, because what is perceived, is.

Rule No. 3: *In the absence of information, we assume*. Whenever individuals are involved in an enterprise that is important to them—and board members fall into this category—as a function of human nature, they will be anxious if they do not understand the reason behind the activity in which they are involved. There is a driving need to know "why." What will happen is that in the absence of knowing the reason for something, a board will make one up.

In a knowledge-based culture, we frequently observe behaviors, opinions, judgments, and decisions based on perceptions that may be founded on incomplete, inaccurate, or out-of-date information which, in turn, was based on assumptions made in the absence of any information at all. But this does not matter; what is perceived, is.

Rule No. 4: *Behavior, no matter how illogical, has a logical base*. The effective leader must work continually to assess the information base serving as the source of perception for the board's behavior or decisions.

To help the board make reasonable, systematic, and rational decisions, the executive must pay close attention to the type, quality, and content of information it receives that serves as its basis for deliberations. That is a legitimate function, not manipulative. In fact, isn't managing information that the association membership and its leadership need one of the executive's primary responsibilities?

Optimum Information Load

In a knowledge-based environment, attention is paid to the "optimum information load" for a board. This relates to how much information is given to a board on a particular issue, how it is formatted, and how it is presented. Optimum information load differs from issue to issue, but there exists a real point at which you have presented your board with the most effective amount of information in the most effective way.

Associations struggle to achieve this point. If a board is given too much information, board members become suspicious because they believe there is something you are trying to hide in the bulk of information. If a board is given too little information, board members will become suspicious because they will think there is something you are trying to hide by not telling them everything.

In a knowledge-based culture, attention is paid to how things are done—not just what is done. Part of the orientation technique, particularly for the new board members, (and if done with new board members the assistance of some of the veteran board members should be enlisted) should be to talk about how the board should go about doing its business. Values and norms should be discussed. Norms represent promises people make to each other that govern behavior. They represent the "rules" of the culture.

The Conflict Corridor

Unfortunately, associations that are not knowledge based invite conflict. They have a set of negative norms. For example, one of the negative norms in the conflicted association is "do unto others before he or she does it to you." Another negative norm of the conflicted association is the assumption of a hidden agenda. Even if there is none there, the assumption is that there is one there. Here, the golden rule is, "He or she who has the gold, makes the rule." A win is defined as another's loss, rather than as two achieving what they both want.

Last, but not least, another norm in the conflicted association is called "the victim's mentality." That is when a group spends most of its time arguing over who should have the power to make a decision and none of its time on what the decision should be. Often, the reason group members do that is to escape responsibility because they perceive themselves as victims. They continually get a message that somebody else has to do the things that need to be done. "We tried the best we could." "You know we are doing the best possible." "It is simply out of our control."

What Board Members Really Want

Boards have the tendency to delegate responsibility, but not authority. This is a hard fact of life in associations, and it is unlikely that it will dramatically change. The best that can be achieved is a willingness by the board to share authority; it seldom delegates it totally. The reason for this stems from the special sense of ownership boards of voluntary associations possess. It is one of the characteristics that makes it very different from any other kind of board in any other kind of enterprise.

Boards often desire maximum control with minimum time involvement. There is nothing wrong with this; in fact, it is a useful guideline to employ in determining how staff can structure its work with the board to satisfy what may be unarticulated but real expectations. This "minimum time involvement," gives executives the space so often needed to get the job done for the board.

CHAPTER 5

Board Members Are People

Frequently, there is a tendency to think of a board of directors or board of trustees as almost a monolithic entity; one that arrives at decisions with minimal dissent, with all its members operating essentially in harmony. If such a board does exist, it is rare because every board is composed of people: individuals with their own reasons for joining, their own desires, ambitions, and fears and, most significantly, their individual characteristics and personalities.

Recognizing such individuality and coping effectively and strategically with any conflicts that might arise will, in large measure, determine whether you will be facing partners or piranhas during your tenure as association executive. What strategies can we employ to overcome deficiencies? How do we orient these volunteer leaders?

Volunteer Self Interest

We should continually ask ourselves whether what we are proposing is going to contribute to a board member's enhanced self-image. Does it run the risk of somehow deprecating or reducing the board member's sense of self? Doing the former can help you learn. The latter can make you a candidate for search and referral.

There are some needs people do fill when they take on volunteer or leadership roles. But, essentially, association executives really have no external currency to use as rewards for them. What operates in associations is "wantivation." Unlike motivation, wantivation comes from the inside. Wantivation occurs when volunteer leaders determine that it is in their own self interest to do the job and do it well. Their own self interest is defined in their terms, not ours.

Here are some of the reasons people volunteer for leadership roles:

- Some people volunteer to use their knowledge or skills
- Some volunteer to give their life purpose and significance
- Some volunteer simply to help
- Some volunteer to be recognized and acquire status
- Some volunteer to feel useful and needed
- Some volunteer to develop their skills
- Some are social joiners who want to participate in enjoyable activities
- Others volunteer to gain competencies and visibility that advances them in their work or in social arenas

- Still others volunteer to use leisure time and reduce loneliness and boredom

All these reasons for volunteering have a common characteristic. In one way or another they contribute to advance board members' self concept and make them feel better about who they are. This is at the core of why they belong to the association in the first place, but it takes on additional significance when they are on the board. This is another crucial insight for the executive. This becomes a guideline in making decisions about what we want to do or want not to do and, more importantly, how we do it.

Examine the many different reasons people become board members. Use that understanding as a stepping stone to explain behavior. Find ways you can influence that behavior appropriately and properly—in service to both the organization and the individual, not simply in your own self interest—although, clearly, you do have one, don't you?

Here is a valuable exercise. Picture in your mind's eye a board member with whom you recently have had the best of all possible experiences. Write down the name. Picture this individual's face. Can you identify in your own mind which of the reasons listed, or what collection of them, is why this person has gotten involved? Next, mentally work your way through each of the other members of your board, and try to assess what is causing them to be there. That is where you are going to look to understand what they perceive to be their own self interest. If you cannot determine the reasons that caused them to invest their time and energy, then, as an executive, you had better find out a bit more about your board members in order to work effectively with them.

The key for an executive to work effectively with the board is understanding the self interest each of those volunteers holds. If you can understand why they are there then you can draw on this interest by creating opportunities for them to realize their self interest and for the wantivation to take place. This is not manipulative or pejorative. It is simply exploiting reality.

Personalities and Preferences

People have preferences. Certainly, they have physical preferences. They also have thinking preferences reflected in their leadership styles. You have probably noticed that some of your colleagues have some leadership styles and preferences that are much like yours, and others have leadership styles and preferences that are different than yours. The culture of a knowledge-based association is sensitive to different thinking and working styles. It values diversity in thinking and is committed to getting full advantage from different perspectives.

A board composed of people with the same preferences may lack either breadth or in-depth perspective in their analyses. This presents the challenge of achieving balance in problem solving.

Mixing Introverts and Extroverts Effectively

Extroverts tend to think and solve problems out loud—you know they are problem solving because you can see their lips moving, and you can almost hear them thinking. An analogy is that their computers are connected on line to their printers. Extroverts often say, "Just let me talk long enough and I will figure out the answer." Introverts typically solve problems differently. They require a short period of quiet time to think about and reflect on a problem before they can discuss it. An analogy is that they need to put their information in batch-storage, review it, and then release it to the printer. Introverts typically say, "If I can just get some quiet time to hear myself think, I can figure out the answer."

Introverts and extroverts do not always mix effectively together to solve problems. Extroverts immediately start talking out loud, and the introverts cannot hear themselves think (just like radar or communication jamming). As a result, the introverts will not interact in the problem solving at all.

Knowledge-based boards must communicate effectively to adequately discuss and arrive at sensible, practical, realistic solutions to the problems the association continually faces. To do that, agreements need to be constructed as to how to work together to make use of the strong points of all the preferences and styles represented on the board. This is an opportunity for colleagues to learn more about each other and about ways to get maximum benefit from their particular personalities.

Here is an example: An extrovert and an introvert working together might agree that the extrovert would listen for a time to the introvert and that the introvert would periodically state his/her thoughts and reflections and talk a bit. Likewise, the introvert would agree to be patient while the extrovert is "thinking out loud." While introverts like an agenda, so they can think ahead about issues that are going to occur at the meeting, extroverts exhibit wide-range thinking where one concept generates another.

Introverts do not like surprises. When sitting at a board meeting they do not like someone to say to them, "We haven't heard from you in two hours. What are you thinking?" That just does not work well. You will not get a good, thoughtful answer. Mutual consideration is the basis for effective communication in all instances.

Many introverts are excellent thinkers and effective talkers, but less comfortable talking, so they hold back. In knowledge-based associations, some emerging virtual technologies, however, are creating more comfortable opportunities for people who are strongly introverted to be involved in conversation. Creating discussion threads using a walled-off part of an association Web page enables introverts to actively engage in deliberation, but at their own pace, with sufficient contemplative time for them to feel comfortable.

If board members are exchanging information by keyboarding, rather than verbalizing, they often find a significant shift in who takes the lead in the conversation. The focus is more on the content being considered and less on eloquence of speech around it.

Board Leadership Profiles

Board members usually demonstrate one of three leadership profiles. One is the achievement-motivated board member who wants to excel, who wants feedback, and who wants challenging work. A second profile is the power-motivated board member who needs to influence others, who desires prestige, and who desires authority. A third is the affiliation-motivated board member who has a need to interact and to feel liked.

Not every board member can be compartmentalized into one or another of these. Most board members, however, do have traits dominant in one of these profiles, and practically every board member demonstrates some aspects of all three. This knowledge is useful when you combine it with an understanding of the styles that different volunteers exhibit.

A challenge facing association leaders is to more creatively construct leadership opportunities that are compatible with the personalities and lifestyles of members. Members should not be asked to reconstruct their lives to be compatible with what they are asked to do. When this happens, leader-members quickly move down the ladder of involvement and become "joiners"—those involved in initiatives but not those who lead them. Then they move from joiners to becoming "belongers," those who may be members but who do not participate actively or use association programs and services consistently. A belonger that stays a belonger and does not move up very soon becomes a non-member. That is called "turnover."

The Leadership Pipeline

Executives should spend some time analyzing the "leadership pipeline" and tracking people as they move through it. In every association there is usually a set of steps people go through to get on the board—this is the leadership pipeline. This exists even in trade associations where board membership is defined in bylaws; for example, "the official of (X) will serve on the board."

There are three things an association may want to do with that pipeline. Make sure people have experiences as they move through the pipeline that will help them develop the kinds of competencies they will need to become the types of board members or officers you seek. Make sure there are opportunities for them to spend time, before they get there, with the "good" board members who have been there. They will learn from the experiences of others. Make sure they are exposed to outstanding and innovative thinkers who will encourage them to want to stretch beyond current common wisdom.

Track their experiences and how they demonstrate competence and willingness as they move through the pipeline. Sometimes, you may have to provide increased opportunities for individuals to demonstrate competence levels more visibly. This allows the responsible body to decide more easily whether to move him or her forward. It may also test an individual before they get into a position where the level or scope of responsibility, if improperly exercised, might cause irreparable harm to either the organization or, of more personal importance, to the executive.

Memberships that have had the opportunity to receive adequate and accurate information, seldom make bad decisions. Mentally healthy people, given essentially the same information, will come to fundamentally similar conclusions. That dynamic applies as candidates move up through the leadership pipeline.

Keep in mind, there is a special skill in coping without getting clobbered. You must learn to lead without getting caught doing so. This depends on your understanding of the real currencies an association executive has, which are information and the ability to construct procedures that provide coherence and consistency as time goes on.

Candidly, there are times when you do not feel like saving people from their own evident, highly vocalized stupidity. At the very least, the critical leaders of the membership are aware of those individuals who may be politely labeled "the articulate communicators." Leadership knows, and will usually find a face-saving way to sidetrack, those individuals before they get into positions to do real harm to the organization.

Leadership Styles

Three kinds of leaders will be examined here. You will probably be able to visualize certain individuals described. How do we match the styles and talents of those leaders with the organization's needs? Why are certain leaders popular although ineffective? On the basis of the answer to that question, how do we make decisions and employ strategies, as association executives, to manage a difficulty or to take full advantage of an opportunity.

The Leader Style

Some volunteer leaders display the leader style. These individuals want an assignment that is large in scope, broad, and long-term. They often seek to exercise power, and not in the pejorative or negative sense, but in the sense of having an impact, an influence over something important.

The Manager Style

Another style is the manager style. These people are looking for an activity that provides an opportunity for large-scope effort, on a short-term basis. They often want to do things, but to be in charge of tasks of short duration.

The Task Style

A third kind of style is the task style. These are the very competent officers and the energetic and committed individuals seeking opportunities to do something small in scope and short-term. Their desire is to do things—to be involved in doing more than managing.

Construct Opportunities That Fit

When you ask volunteer leaders to do something, the question you often get back is "What are you asking for, my money or my life?" Just as often the answer has to be, "Both." Executives must learn to construct opportunities for leaders that fit what they understand about members' styles and profiles.

Remember that leadership pipeline discussed earlier. Board members along that pipeline generally have only one direction to go—up, and traditionally those high offices end year to year. This creates the problem that some board members who are excellent or incredibly committed at lower levels of the ladder are not going to be effective at higher levels. Mismatch!

Now what can be done about that? One thing to do is to reconstruct the reasons people became involved. When a performance problem occurs, the source of that problem usually lies in one of two places. Either it is a problem of competence, or a problem of commitment.

If it is a problem of competence, there are some strategies that can be used. You can try to train or try to coach those individuals, or you can provide some other kind of support to get them through the job.

If it is a problem of commitment, there are other strategies you can employ. You can try to "wantivate" them. Somehow match what it is you are asking them to do to their own self interest to encourage them to handle the task and to do it well. You can counsel or support them.

In your mind's eye, once again, picture an individual with whom you recently had a less than desirable interaction. Based on your perceptions, identify whether the problem was one of competence or commitment.

Helping the Popular but Ineffective Leader

In any situation where leaders exist that are popular and influential but ineffective, there are "driving and restraining forces." The driving forces concern why the person is popular. The restraining forces concern why he or she is ineffective. Since ineffectiveness is due to either incompetence or unwillingness, write down what you perceive to be restraining forces in this board member's behavior. Once you have made your analysis, you have to do some "futuring" (projecting outcomes based on current information, insight about future needs, and intuition about future possibilities) to make decisions about how you will respond.

There are several possible futures for this type of board member. Future one suggests that the board member will, in fact, be able and willing to learn. If competence is the source of the problem, that is probably the future you will seek.

Future two suggests that there is a hidden agenda that needs to be addressed, and what is going on is actually a false conflict. You have to get past it and confront the real agenda. Remember, a good way to do that is to use "what is perceived is . . ." as a mental method of collecting additional information to assess the reality of what is taking place. Executives cannot resolve false conflicts. At best you are pouring oil on troubled waters, and all you will get is an oil slick.

Future three involves a strategy of enhanced role differentiation between staff and volunteer leadership known as enforced support. This might involve asking this individual to do some special things that he or she is good at, or asking other individuals to pick up some responsibility for some of the things that board member is not good at but has as part of his or her assignment. Also, the board member could be further supported by surrounding him or her with either other board members or staff to help accomplish what is needed.

A real example of enforced support occurred at one association that had a president who was from the old school of thought that exemplified the days when associations had executive secretaries. This person truly believed that her responsibility as chief elected officer was to run the organization, as opposed seeing that the organization was well run. There is an important distinction here.

An additional problem was that this individual also believed she was entitled to set policy for the association—on the spot; instantaneously—and within earshot of several important legislative committees! It was agreed that this individual needed a special kind of support known as "insulation and encapsulation." The other members of the executive committee got together and set up assignments for themselves. The result was that this president never went anywhere without another officer along—practically handcuffed together.

There are other ways to provide a flow of information and support. Assign a staff member to provide a constant flow of good information from you to an officer or board member who needs the help. This has its risks but is often an effective strategy.

Another possible future is that exposure, in time, will change others' opinions of the leader. This is particularly important when it involves a leader on the way up. With this prognosis, you have the possibility of three avenues: train the leader, resolve the conflict, or provide opportunities for the leader to demonstrate competence or absence of competence that does not risk irreparable harm to the organization.

Using the Grapevine

People react according to how they perceive reality. Remember the rule, "What is perceived, is?" Here is another example of how that applies.

You can expect your association to have a grapevine. In every grapevine, and every association has one, there are individuals we will affectionately refer to as "key communicators." A key communicator is an individual who appears to have dedicated his or her life to sharing information. That dedication is not necessarily to veracity. That person's dedication is simply to providing information.

What does this person have to do with this dynamic and working effectively with your board members? Recognize that a primary source of available information, second only to your board members' own personal and professional experience base, is those key communicators. Key communicators have as much to do with shaping the vision that the membership and the board have of the organization as does anything else.

Picture in your mind the key communicators on your board—and they are there. Develop a routine, systematic method for ensuring that those key communicators have truth to spread. You will find that they will do as effective a job spreading good news as they do spreading bad. It will not be nearly as much fun for them, but it will still get done. Again, you are not manipulating, you are giving information to a member to help shape a clear, common, positive vision of an achievable future. The only caveat to follow is to make sure that when you use those key communicators, you use them only to spread good news.

If you have a complaint about something or somebody, do not send a negative message into the grapevine. If there is a problem, talk about how to find a solution. Complaints about people have a tendency to loop around and come back to hit you. Use your key communicators, but use them well.

These are not always iron-clad solutions. But they are particularly useful as starting points for sitting down with some friendly partners and making more specific judgments based on things you know about particular personalities you deal with and their agendas that relate to the organization.

Remember there are two separate and distinct, although closely related, areas of effort and concern in the dynamics of the leadership partnership. The first area is orienting and working with your board as a leadership group. The second is focusing more specific attention on dealing with individual board members, be they effective, popular, and/or influential but ineffective leaders. The ways you recognize these two separate areas and select strategies to deal with them will determine whether your board members become partners or piranhas.

A Lesson About Pleasing Everybody

Many years ago there was an executive who managed a relatively small association but one that had many chapters located around the countryside. This was a long time ago, before the internal combustion engine and before mass transportation, and this executive was not paid very much money. (A condition some executives today insist has not changed much in the ensuing years.)

This executive was so poor he could not afford a horse to ride around on; he had to ride around on a donkey. Very embarrassing! This executive's young son came to him one day and said, "Daddy, I know what everybody in town does, except you. I know what the wheelwright does, what the candle maker does, what the smith does, but I have no idea what you, the association executive, do."

The association executive said, "I have an idea. Why don't you go with me as I make my rounds and you can see what it is that your dad does for a living." Well, what child would turn down an opportunity to go to work with its father, mother, or some other significant adult to see what this person does in the course of a day when not in the child's sight?

So the association executive and his young son started out for the first chapter in the first town with the association executive riding astride the donkey and his young son walking alongside. About three miles outside of the first chapter a member of the chapter board came running toward them, screaming and shouting at the top of his lungs, "What a terrible thing you're doing! What a horrible value you're projecting! What will people perceive? This is simply unacceptable behavior on the part of an association executive."

The executive asked, "What is the problem?" The board member said, "Look at this. Here you are, an adult, riding atop the donkey while this poor, young child walks alongside. What does that say about how we, in this association, care about children?" And the executive replied, "You know, you may have a point."

Trying to be responsive to the will of the board member, the executive and his young son headed out to the second town, but this time his young son was riding atop the donkey and the executive was walking alongside. About three miles outside the second town another board member came running toward them yelling and screaming, "What a terrible thing you're doing! What a horrible value you're projecting! This is simply unacceptable behavior on the part of a chief executive officer."

The executive, taken aback, asked, "What now?" And the board member said, "Look at this. What are people going to think? Here you are, our executive officer, walking alongside the donkey while this strapping, young man rides astride. What does that communicate about how we, in this association, respect our elders?"

The executive, being a good executive said, "You know, you have a point." And, being a good executive, he tried once again to respond directly to the will of a board member. This time, the association executive and his young son headed to the third and final town on his rounds, with both of them riding atop the donkey, together. Three miles outside the final town the donkey collapsed under their combined weight, rolled over, fell over a cliff down a precipice, into a pond, and drowned. The executive picked himself up, brushed himself off, picked up his young son, brushed him off, and said, "Son, there's a lesson to be learned here. If you try to please everybody all the time, you're going to lose your ass."

CHAPTER 6

Sustaining a Successful Program Portfolio

Knowledge-based associations, like all associations, must constantly assess and adjust the relevance of programs to make them attractive to current and potential members. Knowledge-based associations, however, tend to do this by navigating effectively through exit barriers (factors preventing the organization from divesting the program) and, as a routine process integrated into strategic decision-making, by anticipating changes needed in the overall program portfolio.

Programs That Decline

Three conditions inevitably cause a program to move into decline:

1. The program was created in the past to meet a need that no longer exists
2. The program was created in the past to meet a need that still exists, however, there is now a far better way to meet that need, and someone else is or could meet it that better way
3. The program was created in the past to meet a need that still exists, and it is being met in the best possible way, however, the proportion of total membership who view the need addressed by this program as a high priority has significantly declined

The Program Meeting No Need

This program is headed down the tubes no matter what you try to do with it. Why in the world does an association continue a program made to meet a need that is not there anymore? The answer is "exit barriers," things that make it hard to get out of a program once into it.

An example of an exit barrier is bylaws committing to a specific program. To abandon the program, the association has to alter the bylaws. Altering the bylaws involves the distribution of power, and then the issue of how the power is changing becomes the focus of attention, not the vitality of the program under question.

Another exit barrier is the "sacred cow" and its champions. This is a particularly tough exit barrier. This refers to a type of program created by a group of deeply appreciated veteran members of the association who are still heavily involved, who happen to be former presidents of the organization, and who possess the ability to communicate with other members.

Somehow they have gotten confused along the way and now view this program as their personal contribution to a better future for the world. They see any attack on the program, any attempt to alter or abandon it, as a personal assault. Nothing causes past leaders to get out to a meeting more quickly than an attack on a sacred cow.

If you start out by saying there is a terrible problem that needs to be fixed, you are going to have some traditionalists who deny that there is a problem at all. Then the argument as to whether or not there is a problem is over. If you start out by saying, "We are doing something wrong; we've got to do it differently," then you are going to have some people defending the way it is being done.

Leaders in a knowledge-based culture learn to position change in a way that does not assault traditional values but, instead, celebrates and acknowledges them and positions the change as their next logical evolution. At that point, with a little luck, you can take at least the critical mass of those traditional leaders and make them some of the strongest sales people for the change.

Another common exit barrier is "staff turf." This takes place in associations that have functional silos in their organization, a condition antithetical to a knowledge-based operational philosophy. Different parts of the staff have constituencies of members, usually standing committees that they support, which take political, defensive positions.

To overcome that, the knowledge-based association moves to a more contemporary staffing structure that gets rid of those functional silos and builds cross-expertise teams within the staff. These teams have responsibilities for outcomes, not programs or functions.

Another frequent exit barrier is dependence on a program as a source of revenue for other activities. There are two intervention strategies here. You must either find another source of revenue to replace it or the association has to stop spending so much money. Those, or some combination of the two, are the choices.

Someone Else Could or Is Meeting the Need Better

A second, more subtle, condition causing program decline occurs when a program was created in the past to meet a need that still exists. However, there is now a far better way to meet that need, and there is someone else meeting it that better way or somebody that could be. In very short order you will find that program headed down the tubes.

You cannot make your existing program work better by altering your promotion of it or by slightly altering the delivery system. Somebody just has a better way of responding to that same need than you have.

If that is the condition, you have two choices for intervention strategies. One is to get out of the business and let the group that is better at it do it, thereby allowing you to focus on the things you do better. The other intervention strategy is cooperation, strategic alliance, and coalition. Find out who the superior competitor is and develop a relationship with them. You might end up marketing its program to your members. Maybe you will share revenue, maybe you will not. Maybe, in exchange, they will market one of your programs to their members.

Look for another group that does different things for the same population or that does the same thing but for a different population. That is where potential allies are found. The knowledge-based association uses awareness of member needs as insight into its capacity and strategic position to focus on its "services niche." Its objective is to make sure that its members' needs are met, not necessarily to always be the place that tries to meet them.

Need Important to Fewer Members

The third, most subtle condition of all causing program decline, and the one most frequent, is when a program was created in the past to meet a need that still exists, and you are meeting the need in the best way possible. However, the proportion of total membership who view the need as a high priority has significantly declined. A much smaller number of members now see this program as being of high value. The program will head down the tubes because of an insufficient economy of scale to maintain it at the level of excellence to which even its historic users were accustomed. It will develop a bad reputation. If the program represents a memorable moment of membership, an internal public relations problem develops as well.

There are two intervention strategies here. One is to find a strategic alliance with another group that can share the cost. Another choice is to piggy-back the program—not to abandon it. Relocate that program inside another that is better supported, or piggy-back it at the front or back of a program that is more viable, thereby redistributing some of the cost of the program by sharing it with the other more successful program.

In associations it is very hard to simply abandon a program in old age. You are really engaged in orderly divestment. One by one, exit barriers must be identified and solved until you are in position to move on.

Knowledge-based associations are realistic and creative. A knowledge-based association needs a critical mass of 20 to 30 percent of its most articulate members to agree to a change that will only be fully understood once you have begun to implement it. If you get this percentage of your most respected members to say "yes," you have sufficient critical mass to build momentum to move ahead.

Take the case of an organization that is half trade association and half professional membership. The difficulty facing this large, historically active association is that the structure of the industry it represents has been severely altered by aggregation and consolidation. Its members are now divided into two primary segments: small members trying to compete in the marketplace by differentiating service and product as a strategy, and larger members, now crossing all the geographic lines used to define the organization, competing on the basis of cost by using economies of scale to deliver a quality product.

Two different membership markets want the association's help. It decides to respond by reorganizing programs and services and by being prepared to do different things for each of these two very different membership markets. To do this, it waives all consistency in its rules about how work gets done. It commits to forming work groups to get particular jobs done and then to allowing those work groups to create their own decision systems, work processes, governance systems, and products, so their assignments and how they accomplish them are a good match. It abandons consistency, recognizing that, in this instance, it is no longer a strategic advantage.

Essentially, it abandons all the bylaws that set rules about who is going to do what, and how they ought to do it. This might be a bit uncomfortable for some of your more traditional members for whom consistency has historically been equated with fairness.

A Case Study

How do you overcome resistance? Here is an example employed by the National Association of Realtors when it confronted this very problem. It began by increasing the confidence of those who would have to be comfortable with a great change in culture, norm, work system, and process, specifically by referring to the organization's history of dramatic change.

In a major, strategic planning conference, a visioning session, they put a time chart up on the wall. The beginning of the time chart said 1980, and the end of the time chart stated the current year. People went up to the wall and listed different points in time where major changes had occurred in the real estate industry and in the Realtor organization. They ended up with 150 significant transitions in that time chart.

The point, made and appreciated, was that the organization had a history and tradition of reinventing itself in major ways when required. Not only did it enjoy a history of being able to do that comfortably, but it rejoiced in that being a piece of their culture. It was something they were proud of. This demonstration of confidence in the organization's competence enhanced the self-esteem of those who had to make the necessary decisions to alter the organization's culture.

Because of segments with different interests in the real estate industry, a compact was developed recognizing there were going to be occasions of disagreement by the segments over certain issues. This also recognized that sometimes the members might go to war with each other outside the association. There is no way to get total agreement preventing that. The only agreement sought, therefore, was that, when going to war with each other over an issue, the organization would not be abandoned during the dispute.

That is not an uncommon dilemma today for many associations experiencing similar positions in the marketplace. With just a little effort you can detect similar, if not identical, dynamics occurring within the constituencies of your own organization. Whether in education, research, public affairs, or public promotion, the same dynamics occur.

Stages of Life of the Association

Like humans, associations go through certain life stages. They are conception, infancy, puberty, young adulthood, adulthood, late adulthood, old age, and, finally, revitalization/obscurity/dissolution. There are many models of these life stages, and there is no universal law dictating their types or sequences. Every association does not automatically move through these stages in a pre-ordained order either, spending a specific amount of time in each stage.

There are many associations whose leadership has somehow managed to move them almost directly from infancy to old age. If that model were displayed more accurately, it would look more like a cycle, because associations go through all these stages, cycling back to the beginning.

Some associations go through them in a spiral, always maintaining maturity, regressing, and then advancing as time passes. With that in mind, it is important to recognize that all associations are apt to exhibit characteristics of more than one of these stages at the same time.

Eight Stages in the Life of an Association

CONCEPTION	A group of people see an advantage to voluntarily coming together and starting an association.
INFANCY	The founders are still in charge as the organization struggles to survive. Every job requires more work than the founders can do.
PUBERTY	The organization grows steadily but suffers awkwardness in its dealings with outsiders and with internal coordination. Entrepreneurial skills are gradually replaced by more professional management techniques and skills.
YOUNG ADULTHOOD	Accepted management practices are implemented, including formalized personnel practices. The beginning of bureaucracy and internal politics are evident.
ADULTHOOD	The organization is mastering its environment and serving the needs of its members. Management is peaking and preparing to expand, to enter new areas of service, or to add new functions.
LATE ADULTHOOD	The excitement of the organization has diminished. The membership will not support innovation. A complacent atmosphere lacking any sense of urgency or zeal prevails.
OLD AGE	The organization is losing its ability to cope with its environment and serve members' real needs. Managers and leaders bicker, and internal control is lacking. All of a sudden things seem to come apart, and few people seem to care.
	REVITALIZATION/OBSCURITY/DISSOLUTION

Not only are associations in certain life-cycle stages, but so are different programs, initiatives, and business lines. Depending on the program, initiative, or business line, attributes of one or more of these stages may or may not be visible. This point is relevant not only to the association as an enterprise, but also to individual programs that exist or are emerging within the organization.

To understand where you are in this big picture, you must divide these eight stages into three phases. The first phase, which extends from conception to pre- and young adulthood, is the developmental phase. A second phase, which extends from young adulthood up to the edge of late adulthood but not into it, is the mature phase. And the third phase, which extends from late adulthood into the great beyond, is the declining phase.

Associations that are able to sustain success usually exhibit certain proportions of their program portfolio in one or another of these phases. A program portfolio is the sum of all the programs and services offered, each one of which may be in a different stage. In contemporary successful associations, anywhere from 20 to 30 percent of the portfolio is in the developmental stage.

A few years ago, the proportion of programs in the developmental phase was far smaller. Five years ago it was 10 to 15 percent. Last year it was 15 to 20 percent. Now it is 20 to 30 percent. The frequency, rapidity, and nature of change, described earlier, accounts for the great increase in the proportion of programs in the developmental stage in successful associations. As members' worlds change, more and more associations are responding to those changes. At the same time, the life-span of programs is decreasing.

Programs with short life spans are called "flash topics." They used to be called "hot topics." "Hot" implies that the heat remains for a while. "Flash" implies it's real hot, but quickly cools. The life-cycle of a program is also getting shorter and shorter, and leaders must manage through change as a function of leadership, not as a task.

In the association that sustains success, from 40 to 60 percent of the portfolio is mature. In an environment of rapid change, the percentage of developmental programs will be larger; the mature will be smaller. If change is only beginning, the percentage of mature programs will be a little larger and developmental a little smaller. The relationship between the state of change and the stage of programs is obvious.

In associations sustaining success, from 10 to 20 percent of programming is, at any point in time, declining. Every association has programs in decline. It is a hallmark of a healthy association, not an unhealthy one. The only associations that have no programs moving through maturity into late adulthood and old age are those associations that are not doing anything new for anyone.

If your organization or a significant program is in the developmental phase, what should your strategic objective be for the organization or for that program? What is the imperative? Stabilize means hold it there. Do you want to keep it there? The strategic imperative is to get it out of the developmental phase and into young adulthood as quickly as possible! A program or an organization that stays in the developmental stage too long loses energy and momentum.

Young adulthood is the first place where a large proportion of members actually get back some tangible benefit from the program. Up to that point you have been heavily investing in the program with no one, or at least very few people, getting any benefit from it. If you are not able to move from the developmental phase to young adulthood quickly enough, by the time you do get out, energy and interest have waned or, what is worse, the need or opportunity being addressed by the program has been replaced by a new one. If, over time, the organization earns a reputation as being a group that gets good programs out just after they are needed, it is unlikely that it will continue to be an attractive place to join.

When associations slide from maturity into decline it is almost always because leadership has failed to manage mature programs. Either a large proportion of the programs began to get too old, or the small proportion of the programs that were of the greatest significance and visibility to members got old.

Fifty percent of programs do not have to go into old age to move the association into decline. If your association's one core program goes into old age, then, as far as your members or prospective members are concerned, your entire association just went into old age.

Memorable Moments of Membership

When members feel that what had been most important to them is now old, less useful, and unattractive, they will transfer that perception to the entire association. This is called a "memorable moment of membership." Members or prospective members have a tangible point of contact with the organization that is the source of information behind the perception leading to their judgment about the overall health of the association.

If all your members depended on your association for the value of educational programming at its annual meeting, but the annual meeting became old, focusing always on the same topics, instructional, and presentation strategies, then membership's view would be that your organization is old. They would take this view despite the fact that the association might be cultivating an extremely attractive virtual reality system allowing members to access educational and learning opportunities off line and off site, at different times and different places.

Let's say members have a constant contact point with your journal, and the journal is highly valued by them. Either it is a source for their feeling of association and community or it is a source of real insight, information, and knowledge about the future. If the journal looks and feels old, even though the content is still cutting edge, then that memorable moment of membership is likely to result in the perception that the organization is headed into decline.

There are three conditions that will cause a mature program to move through late adulthood into old age and decline no matter what you do, and you should not try to stop them. You should anticipate them so you can gradually move organization assets away from that declining program into your mature programs to keep them viable, or move developing programs up to shorten development time.

Associations are notorious for undercapitalizing new ventures. They try to do a multitude of different, new things, all on a shoe-string. As a result, none of them have sufficient resources supporting them to do the right thing well enough and quickly enough. This is a vulnerability inherent in association structure, because a primary source of new ideas and new programs is the committee infrastructure. If the budgeting process is used to set priorities, rather than a longer-term, strategic planning approach, then almost inevitably the response will be political, rather than strategic. The deck of cards you hold has been dealt out to all the different committees hoping that, by doing a little bit for each, everyone will be kept a little happy. However, the reality is that not enough is done for anyone, and everyone is less than satisfied.

In a knowledge-based organization, things that take priority are defined. How is that done? First, you must know what will constitute success. What outcomes are you after? What is your answer to the Cheshire Cat? Then you can decide which of these opportunities is most likely to move you farthest in the most important direction.

Second, criteria like impact, consequence, immediacy, and likelihood of success must be used to make a confident decision about what the priorities ought to be. It is not necessarily your job, as the staff or elected leader, to make this decision, but the organization depends on you to ensure the decision is properly made.

Member Benefit

Associations are formed to benefit and protect members, and any judgment about policy should be premised on how the particular position the association is going to take will benefit a member. Decisions about program strategy or allocating resources must always be characterized by clarity and consensus on the benefits that will accrue to members as a result of allocating resources for those purposes. Absent the focus on outcome and member benefit in an association, a sufficient sense of perceived value by members will not be earned. If members do not perceive value, they will choose not to become involved.

To illustrate: You sight a prospective new member and, as a leader of your association, you want to get him to join, so you tell him about all that will happen as a result of his investment in the organization. What would you tell that prospect that he is going to get if he chooses to join? "Education" is a usual answer. "Well," the prospect says, "Education is great, thanks, but I have to tell you, I'm really fairly well educated. I'm taking graduate-level courses; I'm in a study group; I'm constantly wandering around the Net learning instantly all kinds of stuff that I need. I have a lot of places where I get educated, so while that is interesting to me, I'm not sure that's enough. What else do I get?" "Political representation," is another reply. "Well, that's great," says the prospect, "but I have to tell you that I'm a baby boomer, and I absolutely abandon the notion of representative governance. No one can represent my opinion as well as I can, and I'm not going to give up my ability to make judgments about what's most important to me by giving somebody else an opportunity to sit on a board and make a decision on my behalf. If you want me to be involved, I don't need you representing me. What I need is for you to give me access to the decision makers, who don't know any more than I do, so I can influence their judgment. Thank you."

Insurance programs are a frequent offer. "That's great," says the prospect, "but I have to tell you, my in-law is in the business and, whatever you offer, I'm able to get a little better deal from the family. What else do I get?" "You can do your job better," you desperately respond. "I can do my job better?" says the prospect, "Now you are getting warmer."

Benefits Versus Features

Do you see a pattern in the kinds of things that were suggested as benefits? The pattern is that they were not really benefits. In marketer's parlance, the kinds of things suggested in exchange for membership were "features" of membership. Features do not attract people to membership. Something called "benefits" does.

Here is an example: Education is a feature. But if, as a result of attending a seminar or engaging in an interactive, computer-assisted instructional opportunity using a page on a Web site, or otherwise taking advantage of that feature, a member learns something that allows him or her to do something important better in a shorter period of time, that is a benefit.

Representation is a feature. Yet if, as a result of the representation, a member saves X amount of dollars by being protected from a nefarious operation or receives an opportunity by removal of a barrier that was legislatively established, for that member it is a benefit.

An insurance program is a feature. But if, as a result of that insurance program, a member gets coverage for a potential event that he or she cannot find anywhere else because it is so peculiar to the nature of work that he or she does, that is a benefit.

Think about the brochures and booklets commonly used to describe what associations offer; those sent out saying, "Come to this program because . . . ." What is always on the front cover? Program features. What ought to be there? Benefits!

Beyond "benefits" there is an additional level. Benefits attract members, but "personal benefits" retain members over time. The difference is a subtle but important one.

To illustrate, again: Education is a feature of membership. If you take advantage of a program and learn how to do something important better in a shorter period of time, that is a benefit. If you take that knowledge back to your own world, apply it, and produce additional margin for yourself, create greater satisfaction on the part of your client, execute some responsibility that you have in a better way than you did before, and, because of that, enjoy a personal feeling of success and satisfaction, that is a personal benefit. It is a personal benefit that retains membership over time.

Benefit works at a theoretical level. Access to a benefit means people receive access to an opportunity they value. Personal benefit occurs when they take the opportunity and it makes a tangible difference to them. Benefit occurs when they use a program and learn something new. The personal benefit occurs when they apply what they learned and it really improves their personal status.

There is a third, critical concept important to leaders, one that tends to link together the previous two. This is the notion of commonness: common problems, common needs, and common goals—that is what an association is made of. A successful, knowledge-based association focuses on the enlightened, common, self interests of its members.

Enlightened, Common, Self Interest

What is meant by common self interest? Everyone has a set of self interests, so there is nothing pejorative, malevolent, or evil about them. This is just a statement of human condition. A good case could be made that each member of your association has a strong sense of self interest because, if they did not, they would not have voluntarily taken steps to belong to your association.

Each of your members has a set of self interests that constitutes a menu, upon which items may not appear in exactly the same order. Your members' menus actually comprise the common purposes for which they voluntarily chose to associate with each other. So, you see, the term "association" is not a label without meaning.

What is meant by enlightened, common, self interests? Enlightenment is a concept leadership must understand. It concerns the focus of self interest. There are two dimensions to the notion of enlightenment. The first has to do with the length and height of your gaze. A sense of enlightened, common, self interest is one that looks beyond the limited interest of the moment into the longer-term opportunity or consequence to the membership served.

One of the things that distinguishes the leader's role from roles others in the organization play is the dependency of the organization on him or her to ensure that the association is thinking about tomorrow. Any decision made today about policy, program, strategy, or resource allocation is a decision that must take into consideration, not just the implications of the moment, but also the longer-term implications affecting the vision of the future that has been constructed. When you can answer affirmatively that what the association is doing today will help it get where it said it wanted to go, and that it will not create a future obstacle to its progress, you have an enlightened outlook.

Community Contributions

There is a second dimension of enlightened, common, self interest. This involves leadership's ability to get the organization to look past what it is doing for its members, into what its members, as a result of their membership, are better able to do for the larger community of which they are a part. This is not merely a reference to an altruistic world view or philosophy; this is, increasingly, an item of considerable self interest for successful associations.

Many associations are tax-exempt organizations. In exchange for that tax exemption there is a quid pro quo. In return for some public good that your organization is accomplishing, it is exempted from certain taxes. The idea is that, if you did not perform that particular service, government would have to do it. If government did it, it would have to tax to get the funds to pay for it. Instead, it gets the service free from your organization.

More and more, the extent to which your organization visibly contributes to the public interest is an item of concern for a number of relevant government agencies. Therefore, leadership's attention to enlightened, common, self interest involves, not just considering the future when making decisions today, but also considering the impact of those judgments on the quality of the service provided by your membership to the communities with which they are involved. That is more than just a commitment to a world view; it is also an understanding of a basic dynamic of the not-for-profit community.

Incidentally, it is often better to use the term "not-for-profit" rather than "nonprofit." There are many businesses that are nonprofit. They do not mean to be, but they are. Not-for-profit expresses a sense of purpose.

Associations as Systems

Figure 2 illustrates the next major challenge association leaders and associations are likely to confront through the next decade.

A description of the activity of your association, society, academy, institute, or foundation, in the simplest of forms, would simply be "processing stuff." It is the

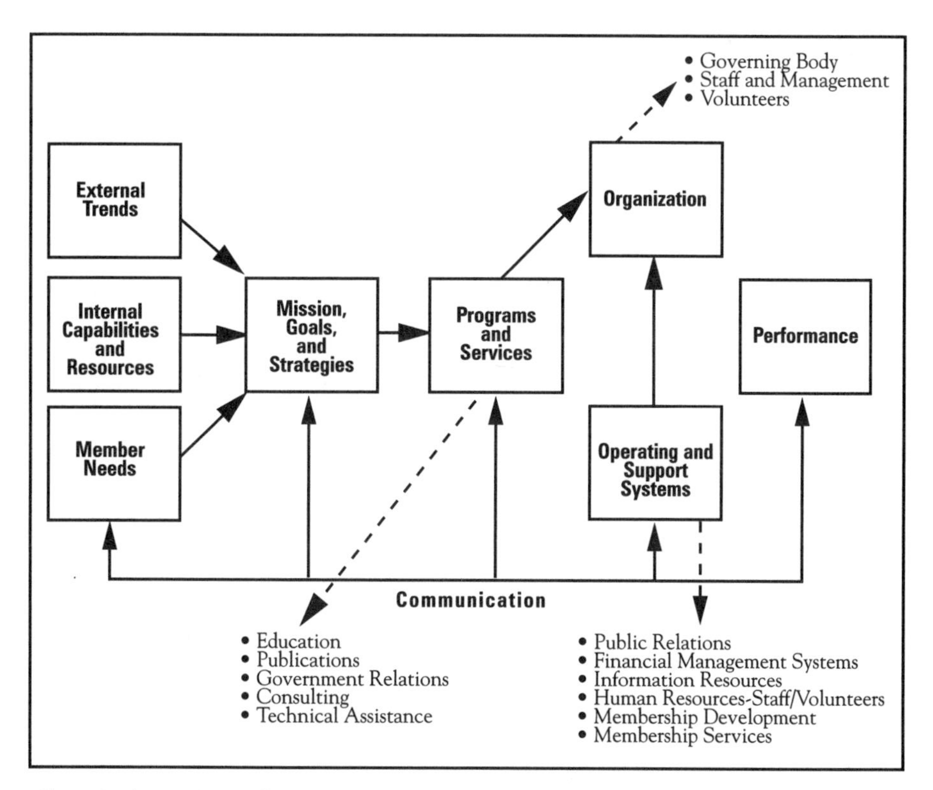

Figure 2. Associations as Systems

nature of the organization that staff executives and elected officers have agreed to ead together. It is, in fact, what occurs in all the various activities that take place in every association.

Here is how it works: Input comes into the association, in the form of data, information, financial or volunteer support, and capacity. The association must then employ processes that transform this data from random information to value-added knowledge, which comes out in the form of products, services, and benefits to members. Now, it is not always that simple. If there are no value-added products or the wrong member benefits come out, the association will tend to attract fewer resources as input (that may be in the form of data, information, financial or volunteer support, and capacity). With fewer resources coming in, there is likely to be less capacity to develop those programs and services members think will constitute meaningful benefits.

Clearly Define What Constitutes Success

Does your association currently face more needs and opportunities than it has the capacity to address with excellence? When demand exceeds capacity, the necessity for leadership to ensure clarity and consensus on what will constitute success becomes paramount. What constitutes success is achieving the outcomes the organization is seeking to achieve and the ultimate benefits sought for members.

If your association suffers from more demand than capacity, then your ability to effectively set priorities becomes absolutely vital. In associations that are not knowledge-based the absence of clarity and consensus on what will constitute success makes setting priorities impossible.

Absent clarity and consensus on what will constitute success, measures of progress cannot be created. If you are not able to demonstrate progress toward outcomes important to members, then it becomes difficult for the organization to maintain its ability to earn perceived value. With no clarity about what will constitute success, and with less capacity than demand and opportunity, your ability to choose among alternatives with confidence is severely diminished. As a result, your credibility as an effective leader is greatly decreased.

Greater Diversity and Specialization

A second dilemma confronts you. Your members are, most likely, becoming less and less like each other rather than more like each other. Even in industries that are consolidating and aggregating, the variety of specialization of focus on either marketplace or product type is rapidly creating increased differentiation among members. In professional societies, as new and different players become involved in the kinds of things that, historically, a more homogenous population had executed, the membership becomes not just larger, but more diverse. As the membership becomes increasingly diverse, their needs, expectations, and preferences also diversify.

Do you see the confluence of the two dilemmas? At the very moment when it is most important for leaders to ensure that they understand what will constitute success, because you are leading an organization in a condition of less capacity than demand and opportunity, two things are occurring that make that difficult to do.

First, the world is changing more rapidly than ever before and, when you think you finally have reached consensus on what is going on, the context changes. Second, your membership is becoming increasingly diversified, so views of what is expected and required are also diversifying at the same time. You are trying to hit a moving target that has a greater number of different, evolving parts than ever before.

CHAPTER 7

Driving Change

Your association does not operate in a vacuum; it operates in a context. That context is characterized, more and more, by rapid, less predictable, significant change. Every time a significant change occurs it has a great impact on your members' needs.

For example, any change in the demography of your members' work force, their marketplace, or the demography of your membership itself, greatly alters their needs. A change driven by government rule, legislation, or regulation that significantly, and sometimes instantly, alters the environment in which your members operate, also alters their needs.

Change is being driven by rapid evolution of computer and communications technologies and the associated hardware, software, networks, and virtual systems used to get work done. When the tools available for members to do their work change, your members' needs and demands on you also become seriously different.

It used to be possible to graph change with a sloping curve called "trends." One could predict that, if something kept going at a steady rate in a particular direction for a specific amount of time, then, at a set point in time, it would end up in a certain place and look a certain way. Today, if you were to graph change, instead of looking like that predictable sloping curve, it would look more like an electroencephalogram. It would have higher peaks and lower valleys than ever seen before, representing new extremes. It would have less space between these extremes, representing more rapid changes.

Even the arena of public opinion suffers from this escalation of highs and lows and from the rapidity with which serious change occurs. That is meaningful for associations, since, for most, public opinion is a very important arena, and advocacy is an important business line.

Constructive and Destructive Change

Leaders of knowledge-based associations recognize that there is more than one kind of change. In the eyes of members there are at least two kinds of change: one is constructive, the other is destructive.

Constructive change is ultimately in the best interest of those affected. Destructive change is ultimately not in the best interest of those affected. Note the value judgment involved in this determination. Whose job is it to decide whether the change is or is not in the best interests of those affected?

The answer is you, the association leader. In fact, a value-laden judgment is what you are most likely to be remembered and held accountable for. A dilemma for leaders occurs, however, when a change is promoted or caused by the external environment, and that change could have differing effects on different segments of your membership. Here, very thoughtful and sensitive judgments become the order of the day, and stakeholders beyond those in leadership should be brought into the decision process.

Let us examine a constructive change. When change in an association is constructive there are three possible responses to what is proposed: Support, neutrality, and resistance. However, in an association, there is really seldom an opportunity for neutrality.

For example: There is something in your bylaws or your policy that says certain kinds of critical conditions require a certain level of majority to be approved. In some cases, the bylaws require agreement of more than 50 percent of those present and voting. If this is one of those cases, and someone chooses not to say "yes" to a proposed change and withholds their vote, is that person supporting or resisting? They are actually supporting by not voting. They are letting the count of those present and voting in the affirmative be higher, so they are actually supporting while refraining from participating.

On the other hand, what if your bylaws say that, on this particular kind of issue, three-quarters of the members of the board must approve, and someone chooses not to vote? Is that support or resistance? It is resistance because you have to count the "yes" votes as a proportion of the total number of the board, regardless of how many vote. There are seldom situations where there is true neutrality in the organization.

Overcoming Resistance to Constructive Change

Resisting constructive change in an association, especially when the change is being promoted by external occurrences over which you have little or no control, is usually caused by anxiety stemming from fear of the unknown. In an association, when leaders encounter resistance to constructive change, it is seldom a result of people disagreeing with what is being proposed. The resistance, as opposed to disagreement, usually comes from people who do not know the answers to two critical questions. These are "What will things be like if the change occurs?" and "Will I be able to handle it?"

Facing Question One

The first is "What will things be like if the change occurs?" Your objective, as a leader, is to create knowledge that overcomes the unknown and increases the resistor's comfort in what things will be like. If you can do this, you begin to melt the resistance. Whether the change will be good or bad is a totally different issue. Your strategy should be to create for them as tangible as possible a vision of how things will be. If you can help them figuratively wrap their arms around the change by using an anecdote, a metaphor, a simulation, then you can expect a measurable increase in the possibility that their answer to the question, "What will things be like?" will be positive.

Suppose, for example, as a leader of an association, you are trying to get staff and elected leadership to use virtual technologies more as a way of getting work done. The association has a board that meets for two weeks every two months to manage the organization. You want to decrease the cost to the organization and to the individuals, in terms of both time and dollars, by getting the group more comfortable with using a piece of their Web page. Using a pass code to get in to look at what the board does, you determine that at least 40 percent of what the board discusses are things that could be deliberated between meetings using computers and communications software. A constant conversation could be facilitated by somebody that would not require someone to be physically present all the time. Everyone says "yes" to the concept. You buy the software and the hardware, give it to everyone, and train them how to use it. But you still do not see movement; you see resistance to the change. How do you solve this problem?

One possible solution is to, at one of the meetings, take all the members of the board, put them in different rooms, and have them use that software and hardware and the network linking them to actually engage in a deliberation just as if they were in different places instead of in the same building.

This would create a simulation allowing the board members to, figuratively, wrap their arms around the new technology, thereby increasing their comfort level. Your objective was to increase their comfort. Your strategy was to provide a tangible vision of what things would be like. As a result of this exercise, the first time they use this setup at home will not be the first time they actually worked that way.

Keep two things in mind. First, there is no single, comprehensive strategy for navigating through serious resistance. The example above was simply to help you better understand the dynamic. Second, the response to resistance to change in a knowledge-based association is using and disseminating knowledge, again, relative to the four key knowledge-based considerations:

- Foresight about the industry or professional future helps construct the vision you share
- Sensitivity to member's views of the world helps you select the language and examples that will be meaningful to them
- Insight into the capacity and strategic position of the association helps you decide the proposed response to a change is appropriate; it also helps you decide how the association is best equipped to help its members
- Consideration of the ethical implications of choices is part of the dialogue that precedes the organization's deliberation in which commitment to the response to change was authorized

Facing Question Two

"Will I be able to handle it?" This is a more personal and subtle question and, for that reason, a question often more difficult to respond to successfully.

Most associations have cultures that are at least somewhat political in nature due to the processes used to select their leadership. In such organizations there is frequently a tendency to misconstrue this question when it is posed. If misconstrued as another question, it yields a different answer than the one required. In a political environment it is often thought the question being asked by the resistor is, "What's in it for me?"

But that is not really the question in resistance. The question actually is, "Will I be able to handle it?" If you misconstrue the question you can come up with a collection of answers about what they are going to get out of it. The resistance will still be there, however, because the real source of anxiety is the issue of whether or not they will be able to handle the change. Your objective, in responding to this source of resistance, is to increase the resistor's self-esteem, whether it is an organization or an individual.

Even in trade associations, where members are organizations, it is still people who represent the organization. Human dynamics are still a big piece of what is going on, even though, technically, the member is an institution. Your objective is to increase their self-esteem because that makes it more likely that their answer to the question, "Will I be able to handle it?" will be "Yes."

Leaders are vulnerable when they mix benevolence with arrogance. Sometimes they think they need to use whatever power they have, and shove change down everyone's throat. That approach decreases the self-esteem of the resistor. What is more damaging to self-esteem than having a sense that something important to you is completely out of your control?

Taking that approach, particularly in a voluntary organization, diminishes self-esteem and increases resistance. The messages here are that (1) despotism, no matter how benevolent, is counterproductive when trying to overcome resistance to change, and (2) in a knowledge-based association information is exchanged, not withheld, as a strategy for addressing resistance.

Key Drivers of Change in Associations

Most primary influences on associations come from the industry or profession they are serving, so each organization represented has a specific set of issues driving change within it. At the same time, however, there is another set of issues that is generically important to all associations. This concerns the commonality of the nature of an association as an enterprise.

Research undertaken by the Foundation of the American Society of Association Executives (1995) sought to identify the key drivers of change, to examine the trends related to those drivers, to make some assumptions about the meaning of those trends, and then to suggest what the implications were for the Foundation.

The research identified the key drivers of change as technology, volunteer leadership, governance and structure, ethics and image, and regulation and legislation. The first three have strong relationships to each other.

Technology

Technology is advancing rapidly and members have high expectations for sophistication. An association's technology is a two-edged sword. It can be either a source of competition that puts it out of business or it can be a source of opportunity that lets it reinvent itself in a way that makes its value to members superior to what it was before. This is particularly true for associations that have primary business lines involving education and information.

Technology does not only create the opportunity for members to enjoy increased access to the intellectual capital that is the primary value of membership for them. It also generates opportunities to accomplish work for groups of people who find it hard to get together at the same time.

One may assume that not all technology will be appropriate for associations; that it will become more user friendly, less costly, and that it will change constantly, and that association members will expect their association to be proficient and sophisticated in its use. The demand on your association to use technology will be directly proportional to the extent to which it is employed by members in their own workplaces and personal lives.

You face a three-part dilemma. The expectation for increased use of technology by the association is high. The degree to which your members can confidently, competently, and capably use technologies is moderate and widely diverse. The extent to which members are willing to provide funds to pay for it is still relatively low. Your ingenuity and experience should help you migrate through these conditions.

What do you do when you know the application of technology is an essential ingredient of your future success, and you want to get started but only a relatively small proportion of your membership enjoys the sophistication, the confidence, and even the technical capability to take advantage of it. Do you make the commitment or not?

Associations committing to a knowledge-based philosophy will discover they have no choice but to take the plunge. Unless you begin the journey to becoming a technology user for communications, marketing, and managing databases; for providing access to the intelligence and knowledge resident in members and staff, and for altering the work systems you use to make decisions—then, in very short order, somebody else is going to come along and use it in a way that supplants you. You have little choice but to begin the journey, regardless of how many members can take advantage of communications technology at the moment.

A practical fiscal philosophy is to use dues to subsidize opportunities for members to use new technological tools. All members are given the opportunity to use them, but those who do pay a fee for use. Then, those members who do not use them do not feel they are unfairly subsidizing those that do. This creates a reasonable balance, in most situations, that allows an organization committing to knowledge-based professional systems to begin the journey.

The implications are that associations will have to increase investments in technology and in training leaders to use it. Driven by your members' expectation that your association will become more proficient and sophisticated in using technological tools, managers will need greater knowledge of how technology can be used in decision making and in member service.

Volunteer Leadership

The second driver of change, volunteer leadership, is related to the first in many ways. It has become difficult for our most talented members to be actively involved in association work. There is no dearth of people willing to volunteer for leadership, but there is a limited supply of "talented" leadership.

There is a huge danger to associations that are unable to devise strategies that encourage the most intellectual and influential members of their industries or professions to be active. The danger is that, in a relatively short period of time, the real drivers of the profession will reside outside the association.

One strategy is to employ technology in a way that permits people to be actively involved without having to travel or to incur the costs of airfare, trains, cars, and hotels. They are able to be there without having to spend time getting there.

There are a variety of technologies emerging, increasingly affordable and easy to use, that offer potential strategies to this impasse. Some very high-powered executives resist using computer-assisted, group-decision software because of keyboard phobia. They can be reassured that clickable options and integrated voice, data, and video communications are creating computer-assisted environments that allow the kind of personal communications that they tend to prefer when dealing with complicated issues involving "trust."

The trend toward increased competition for talented volunteers' time will continue and intensify. Leadership in an industry or profession may not reflect or depend on leadership in that industry's association. More frequently, association staff will be called on to do what volunteers used to do. Already, there is a significant shift of work load to association staff from formerly member-active groups—a shift in paradigm.

Several associations already have moved to using committees of members that report to staff. The role of these committees is to consider and advise, but the role of the staff is to make and execute decisions.

Think about an education advisory committee whose members are on line with each other, maintaining a continuous dialog about needs, expectations, and interests. They are constantly engaged in electronically-based, facilitated conversation about whether a particular learning opportunity will be attractive or not to members. They are asked to consider suggestions, ideas, and alternatives, and float back their own reactions as well as their appraisals of how others in the organization might behave. This way, the staff member responsible for selecting, deciding, and designing has the constant benefit of that continuous, electronic focus group.

Consistent with a knowledge-based operational philosophy, who makes the decision is far less important than the quality of information and insight on which the decision is made. A politically correct committee that makes a stupid decision is not doing anything that benefits anyone.

Associations unable to use technology as a tool to increase organization participation by their most talented members diminish the intellectual capital of the organization. Such groups eventually become comatose and totally unable to absorb ideas or impressions.

Governance Structure

As changes in governance structure, the third driver of change, occur, there should be shifts in responsibility, followed by shifts in authority. The implications for knowledge-based associations are many. New roles and structures have to be defined for both staff and volunteers; association executives have to do a better job of streamlining and facilitating decision making; volunteer training and orientation become more critical; and association management needs to improve and target communication methods to a variety of key stakeholder groups on essential issues.

A paradigm shift is a change in the context used to understand things, and two important paradigm shifts occurring here affect every association. They are no less potent than the shift in thinking, from 1960 to 1990, about America's economic positioning in a global marketplace, or changes from mainframe to network computing, or the shift from radio to television.

One shift is that associations have the opportunity to become increasingly democratic, while at the same time becoming increasingly efficient. In the old paradigm, that would represent a paradox, but technology today allows any association to touch base with each member every day if it wishes to and if members want it to. Most do not, but the opportunity to increase the breadth and depth of participation, in a time where less discretionary time is available, is one knowledge-based associations will not ignore.

The other shift is in the political model for associations. The chief executive of an association in the 1950s and 1960s often held the title "executive secretary." In the 1960s and 1970s the title was elevated to "executive director." In the 1970s and 1980s the title grew to "executive vice-president." In the 1990s, this title often becomes "president" and the elected partner is titled "chair of the board."

A consultative partnership model has emerged, replacing the traditional model emphasizing the employee/employer relationship in associations. Each partner is now viewed as bringing a special kind of expertise and perspective to a discussion where the best decisions are always made by the confluence of both perspectives. Neither can operate well without the other. The knowledge-based association reshapes its systems, structures, processes, and culture to acknowledge this new model and to harness its full potential.

This causes a significant shift in how executives communicate with each other and with their partners in leadership and on the board, and, also, how elected and staff leaders communicate with their members. Improving how associations communicate with their members will determine to a great extent the level to which the organization will be attractive to tomorrow's potential members. These potential members tend to define enfranchisement as active involvement in the dialogues from which decisions emerge, not as having a person like them representing their "interests" on a committee or board.

Attracting Tomorrow's Members

As discussed earlier, for many years, common wisdom correctly held that the primary determinant in the decision to belong to an organization was the extent to which individuals perceived a good match between the programs and services offered and what they considered to be their greatest needs. When the association wanted to attract a new population to membership, it would construct a new set of programs and services designed to respond to their needs. If it wanted to increase the involvement of a segment of already-active members, it would manipulate, massage, and modify its program portfolio to increase its attractiveness to them.

The key to membership development tended to be program manipulation. This does not mean this is not an important factor to someone deciding whether or not to join; it still is. Recent research conducted by Tecker Consultants (Tecker and Fidler 1993) for its clients strongly suggests that a second decision-determinant is emerging related to the judgment to join. Among tomorrow's potential members, the extent to which the organization projects an image of commitment to a set of values with which the individual would be proud to be affiliated, appears to be as important as program manipulation. If the organization's culture is perceived to be unattractive, then regardless of the efficacy of the match between programs and their needs, they are going to go somewhere else.

Along with this shift in decision-determinant comes the very different view of what representation and enfranchisement means to the baby bust generation. The pre-boom, World War II, and depression generations strongly believed in the concept of representative democracy. To them, being represented in the association meant having someone serving on the board or other committee who, demographically, was like them. As long as they saw that, faith in representative democracy allowed them to feel comfortable that they were sufficiently involved and enfranchised.

Tomorrow's members do not view the world the same way. Tomorrow's members view enfranchisement and involvement as requiring their continuous personal involvement in the constant exchange of information from which decisions are made. Having someone else represent them is no longer so satisfactory.

In a knowledge-based association these two relatively new realities are linked to technology, which creates the opportunity for each individual to be actively engaged in exchanging information from which judgments emerge. Where a knowledge-based decision style is used, this is part of the dialogue preceding deliberation—it is part of becoming enlightened about the basis of opinions before selecting from them and using that insight in the deliberation that produces a decision. That is what communication means now.

Associations are being asked to make more complex decisions more rapidly than ever before. This trend will continue and accelerate. The current structure and governance systems of many current associations, however, are obsolete and unwieldy, and they will have to change or they will no longer remain competitive. According to the ASAE Foundation report (1995), one possible, unwanted result of this for associations, is that fluidity, rapidity, and responsiveness in decision making could be a down side to effecting positive change in an organization by disenfranchising members if involvement is lessened as a result. The knowledge-based association avoids that consequence by effectively reshaping structure, function, and processes to create efficiency while preserving, or usually expanding, involvement.

CHAPTER 8

Change: The Only Certainty

For association leaders, the world of their constituents is increasingly characterized by instability and unpredictability. Resistance to change discussed earlier is also apparent, driven not by disagreement about the future that may be coming but by anxiety and fear of the unknown.

The organizational conditions in associations that are not knowledge based are often uncertainty over vision of the future and confusion about appropriate direction. There is continuing conflict and confrontation among increasingly diverse subconstituencies within their memberships over appropriate strategy and style. There seems to be no visible evidence that these conditions will get any better in the foreseeable future.

The conditions affecting governance of traditional organizations are changing dramatically and, because of that evolution, the attitudes, skills, and capabilities of successful association leaders in the twenty-first century will have to be different, more complex, and able to withstand more demands than ever before. (See Tecker and Fidler 1993.)

What are the forces reshaping these organizations? What is the nature of the shifts in their character, and what will be the specific implications for organization leaders into the twenty-first century?

Trends Reshaping Associations

There are five key trends reshaping associations.

1. The nature of change itself
2. Increased demand for outcome accountability
3. Volunteers looking for minimum time involvement, maximum influence, and major benefit
4. Technology's promise, possibilities, expectations, and realities
5. A greater degree of generational and multi-cultural diversity within members' industries and professions, among association work forces, and among members

Change Itself

In earlier days, before the late 1970s, change was much more continuous, predictable, and, arguably, somewhat more manageable. In today's world, change itself has altered in three dramatic ways.

First, it is more rapid than ever before. Second, it is increasingly less predictable than ever before. Third, it is more complex; it is much less sequential and much more the result of a confluence of phenomena, events, activities, and dynamics, many of which are unforeseeable at the same time.

Outcome Accountability

The second major trend reshaping associations is increased demand for outcome accountability. There used to be a time when the executive could be comfortable if he or she wrote a plan, promised to follow the plan, and then followed it. That is no longer the case.

Today's members no longer accept a commitment to activity as a sufficient indication of our commitment to them. It is not enough to build and follow the plan; now what our members look for is demonstration that the plan, once executed, really worked.

Leaders of knowledge-based associations are able to focus on benefits that accrue back to those served as a result of organizational participation. This, however, is tempered by two complexities. One is that what may be defined as a benefit by any member will more likely be different from what is perceived as a benefit by another member. Members are becoming less and less like each other rather than similar to each other. It becomes necessary for association leaders to broaden their consensus of what constitutes success, that is, to be able to agree on where it is they are going and why they are trying to get there. This becomes more and more challenging as the nature and types of demands become more voluminous and diverse.

The second complication is that, again, increasingly, the decision to join a professional organization is based on the extent to which the potential member perceives the organization's culture to match his or her values and to project an image that he or she would be proud to be a part of.

Volunteers: Minimum Time to Invest for Maximum Benefit

The third major trend involves volunteers. The very definite, measured trend is that members are making three demands on their associations because they have less time to give than ever before. They appear to be looking for minimum time involvement, maximum influence, and major benefit. Given the current condition of their personal and work life, that is not surprising or unwarranted.

Technology's Promise

The fourth of the five key trends reshaping organizations is technology's promise, possibilities, expectations, and realities. The tools for us to communicate with, to involve, to create participatory decision making, and to develop and design activities are emerging in a more and more sophisticated environment and at a more rapid pace. This also creates a paradox for leaders. While the expectations and demands of members about how technology is used to make their involvement productive are increasing, their willingness to support the investment necessary to provide this is not yet growing at a compatible pace.

More Diversity

The fifth of the five key trends reshaping associations is the advent of a greater degree of generational and multi-cultural diversity. This is taking place within memberships' industries and professions, among association work forces, and among members.

Members' moods and expectations are becoming different on the basis of variables like the amount of time they spend in their professions, the nature of their roles or professional specialties and subspecialties, the level of industry structure in which their organizations reside, and the site or nature of the organizations in which their work takes place. All these factors are being superimposed on top of increasing diversity. There exists more differentiation resulting from gender-related experiences, generation-related experiences, and other socioeconomic and psychological ingredients.

Character Shifts in Associations

In the face of all this, it becomes increasingly important to maintain clarity and consensus on what will constitute success in an organization. That is, to maintain agreement on what we are trying to accomplish within the environment characterized above.

If you recall, when Alice met the Cheshire Cat in Lewis Carroll's *Alice in Wonderland*, she had come to a fork in the road and asked, "Which of these paths should I take?" Without hesitation, the cat said, "Where do you want to go?" Alice said, I really don't know where I want to go." The Cheshire Cat responded, "That's still an easy answer; either path will do."

That answer might have been appropriate in *Alice in Wonderland*, but in our "Wonderland" it is unacceptable. In a knowledge-based enterprise we maintain clarity and consensus on where we are going and what constitutes success. This is so we know which strategies on a menu are the best to select in order for us to evaluate our progress as the plan unfolds, in order to make adjustments, and to demonstrate achievement of the outcomes our members believe to be worth investment of their time and dollars.

These trends and conditions are causing several shifts in the basic character of associations. A knowledge-based association is constantly aware of the changes in its context that may require adjustment in mission, goals, or strategy. Such paradigm shifts suggest that there is a whole new, evolving world to be aware of. The knowledge-based operational philosophy positions associations particularly well to continually adjust to such changes. For example, changes driven by new needs and demands are already occurring in association structures and orientation, governance, decision making, programming, service delivery, and focus.

Becoming Global

The first shift is in the movement from territorial to global: this is represented by changes in traditional market segments, interdependent economies, and expanding international opportunities. These foretell significant changes in the geographic parameters that historically have defined the interest, membership, and structure of associations.

Role Changes

A second change is in role: a movement from enforcer to consultant, recognizing (1) expanding member needs for usable knowledge, (2) increasing diversity in a larger world and in our memberships, and (3) member demands for greater return on their investments. This suggests significant changes in all levels at all associations, as well as significant changes in the roles our members ask us to fill and how we interact with our subparts.

What this portends, clearly, is that knowledge-based associations will need to redirect their energy from enforcing the rules of membership. Instead, they will need to focus on assisting members to accomplish their desired outcomes.

Governance

A third shift in paradigm is a change in governance approach: It will move from political oligarchy to greater market sensitivity in an increasingly complex marketplace and workplace. Our continually diversifying membership requires decision making at all levels of organization to be based more on accurate, defensible information about the membership and its world, and less on the views of small, insulated groups who are opinion rich and information poor.

There is growing need to achieve demonstrable results in the face of an increasingly diverse set of needs. It is increasingly important to maintain clarity and consensus about what constitutes success within a constantly changing environment. Knowledge-based associations are able to reach consensus by first determining how commonly desired outcomes can best be achieved. They must realize that lowest-common-denominator decision making will become an ineffective approach.

Looking back, we see that, historically, the grandparent associations of North America have employed a political model of decision making borrowed from government. It was borrowed from government because, at the time associations committed to being democratic, there was only one apparent way to tap into the views, experiences, expertise, and values of members.

Here is that probable scenario. All the blacksmiths in San Antonio, for example, would gather at the Alamo Tavern. They would have a few drinks and talk about the issues confronting them. After a few more drinks, they would create an agenda that they would work on. Then they would develop some strategies for implementing the agenda. They would finally take some positions on the issues confronting them and pick one person who would then be assigned to ride to Austin. There, this person would represent all the blacksmiths who were at San Antonio, together with blacksmiths from other parts of Texas, and then all would repeat that same pattern.

At Austin, they, again, would physically gather in one place, talk about the issues, and define an agenda. Then they would pick one person to ride or take a train to Chicago or Washington where, physically, they would all gather and repeat the same pattern.

At that time, there really was no choice but to organize and conduct business that way. It was the only way to gather data needed about members' wants, needs, expectations, and demands. But now, entering the twenty-first century, while there are other ways to communicate with members, the structure of associations and their approaches to governance have not deviated substantially from that original model in 210 years.

Decision-Making Models

Another dimension of what associations have inherited, which does not match tomorrow well, is the political model of decision making. Here the lowest common denominator is usually the basis for an agreement.

With the political model of decision making, we tend to take the worst elements provided by all and combine them. We get an agreement at that point where at least one more than 50 percent of those present and voting do not object to any part of the package. While this model did, and may still, work well for advocacy efforts, it is increasingly ill suited for decisions being made by associations that also provide products and services.

Members are now demanding that our decision making become less like government and more businesslike. We must first reach consensus on outcomes, select from alternative strategies the strategy that appears most effective to achieve the desired outcome, and then make decisions about who is to contribute in what ways to achieve that outcome.

The balance between legitimacy of the decision group and the credibility of the decision is shifting. Where association leaders were formerly primarily concerned about the political correctness of the composition of the group being asked to make a decision, they are now as much concerned about the expertise, experience, and relevant knowledge of the group being composed to make the decision.

This is not a choice; members are demanding a better balance between representative political correctness in the composition of decision-making groups, and appropriate, sufficient knowledge and credibility from those in the group. They must have the experience and perspective, not merely to reach agreement on what to do, but they must be able to define the right thing to do. For organization leaders, the knowledge-based enterprise offers an environment more conducive to responding to these new needs.

Programming Changes

Another shift in the paradigm is a change in programming. The rate and amount of change and diversification in the marketplace, work force, community, and membership requires association programming philosophies to be significantly altered. Large initiatives with diffused relevance to any particular group are increasingly less attractive in most associations.

This suggests, that for most organizations, it will be more strategic to offer fewer programs of higher value to more targeted populations. An accompanying consequence of this strategy is that organizations within a community that previously tended to view themselves as competitors are advised to view themselves as potential cooperators and collaborators.

The cost of competing among associations is usually greater than any association can bear for any significant period of time. Any dollar spent competing is a dollar that cannot be spent delivering quality or breadth of program.

As knowledge-based associations carefully define their service niche—that special match between essential needs of members and what the organization is strategically well-positioned to provide best—they will find themselves engaged in a greater variety of strategic alliances with other groups. This will be done to ensure that the quality and breadth of programming is not compromised in terms of access to members as each seeks to more sharply focus their respective niches.

Delivery System Shifts

A related shift in the paradigm is a shift in service delivery systems from mass to customized. Increased segmentation, rapid change, and member demand for value for their investment, all will require many associations to convert their collective resources into customizable packages. This means most knowledge-based organizations will reconfigure themselves to function as a pool of resources for members they are well-positioned to serve.

Many members do not really care who meets their needs. Their concern, driven by anxiety over an unknown future, is simply that their needs be met. As the future that affects the environments in which they work continues to unfold, they will be expecting needs to be met that, today, we cannot envision. In face of this, the knowledge-based association's ability to remain fluid and flexible is crucial.

Altered Focus

Here is what we may expect in the time to come. Our basic focus will alter. There will exist increased demand to concentrate organization resources on achieving results and greater intolerance of internal political agendas and bureaucracy. All this indicates that, in the twenty-first century association, we will need to redirect our attention from internal affairs to the work that actually must be accomplished. As associations become more involved in meeting the existing and emerging needs of members, they are likely to become more influential in affecting industry, profession, and issue dynamics.

If association leaders do this well, associations will become much more influential players in their areas of interest. That, in turn, should make them increasingly attractive to and appreciated by members.

How a knowledge-based association will construct an identity for itself compatible with these shifts in context will differ from organization to organization. Be wary of anyone who suggests there is one right way to do this—they may be either ignorant of the realities of the situation or trying to sell something on their political or programmatic shelf.

Structural Shifts for Associations

Recognizing that sameness and consistency will no longer be strategically attractive values, there are some generic directions in which associations are moving to reposition themselves for a knowledge-based future. These are driven by the change in the nature of change itself. They are apparent in the alteration of our structures and decision processes.

The strategic direction of our structures is toward greater fluidity. For associations operating in environments where they cannot, with any degree of certainty, predict who the key players in the industry will be, fluidity in structures becomes essential.

"Structures" refers to membership structure, governance structure, program structure, work force structure, financial structure, and information structure. Three strategic directions characterize the nature of the changes occurring within these structures. They are fluidity, flexibility, and responsiveness.

Fluidity

Here is an example that illustrates fluidity in structure. If you have ever bought a pencil and piece of paper, you have had contact with the office products industry. For many years that industry was, for the most part, composed of independent "mom and pop" stores. Larger groups were formed when a few mom and pop stores formed some sort of partnership alliance and had three or four stores in the area. Then this industry, as described, formed an organization called the "National Office Products Association." Activity in the membership structure consisted of the office products store owners of one town meeting with the office products store owners of other towns and selecting one person who would then represent them at the national organization. Sound familiar?

The group also had a governance structure designed so all the different interests of the office products industry were represented around the table, but those interests were defined by geography. It had a program structure that included activities, information, publications, technical assistance, a trade show, and conventions all primarily designed for the mom and pop office products store owner.

It had a work force structure that combined volunteers and professional staff. Primarily, though, its work was driven by a group of committees that were volunteer or member intensive. Each committee had representation from all levels of the organization and all geographic territories. Staff, for the most part, served as glorified clerks to members who were engaged in work on activities about which they had little or no expertise.

The financial structure was composed of a dues system, where each mom and pop store paid dues annually based in part on its income. The members felt this was very progressive.

The organization had an information structure that was very direct. A few people at the top would make decisions in an insulated place and then give some instructions to the people underneath about executing the programs. This often was a link to direction that staff could not understand.

Overnight Change

This was the office products industries association until, almost overnight, Staples, OfficeMax, and Office Depot came along and took control of most of the industry's market share within one year.

The old National Office Products Association now had a problem. None of its structures even had a place for these new industry leaders. They could not even belong. The national association could not figure out how to deliver programs to them and did not even have any way to identify how these major players might participate in dialogue or deliberations.

The organization realized it needed to construct greater fluidity in its membership. It abandoned all its old rules and created new opportunities for people to decide whether they would become members or not, rather than have the organization define who its members would be. This is an example of a shift in paradigm where the marketplace decides whether and how it wants membership, rather than the organization deciding whether the individual can be a member or not. This demonstrates fluidity in structure.

The fluidity occurred just in time, because, just as these big players could finally become members and get active in the organization in ways that were meaningful and useful to them, some business product suppliers are intending to sell products in grocery super-stores. And why not? Thirty percent of America now spends a big percent of its time working at home. It is expected that, in another five years, fully 50 percent of America will spend an even larger percent of its time working at home. In that case, why should you not be able to go to any supermarket, walk down one aisle for your breakfast cereal and, in the next aisle, pick up that floppy disk you need for the afternoon?

If, as little as five years ago, someone would have suggested to the leadership of the National Office Products Association that its members might shortly include the executives of a supermarket chain, you can guess what the response would have been. They can belong to the association and participate where there is a congruence of interest.

Flexibility

The second shift, therefore, in this paradigm, is in flexibility. This involves finding ways to be more flexible as organizations, to be more able to easily move assets around, to reshape, and to move much more quickly.

Again, consistency and sameness, in terms of decision systems, information systems used to make those decisions, and work processes, used to be strategically attractive. This was because these were viewed as ways to achieve fairness among different groups and parts of an organization.

Inevitably, sameness and consistency will prove more and more disadvantageous to associations' success. In a world of diverse needs, flexibility and how associations organize to meet needs becomes strategically important. How the work gets done must match the kind of work required; and, of course, the kind of work required will differ depending on the specific need or objective. Approaches to processes within an association will become vastly different.

How will associations become more flexible? Work groups will be specifically constructed to deliver programs, products, or services responding to particular needs. The composition of those work groups, their decision systems, and the information systems they use to make those decisions and to develop their work processes will be entirely different from those of other units or parts of the organization.

For association leaders, managing that new flexibility will require new perception, competencies, and attitudes. A knowledge-based culture will be essential.

Responsiveness

The third change associations face is movement to responsive structures. Associations must become able to move more quickly. The world does not hold still for traditional governance processes based on the political model.

Remember, the American government model was originally constructed to prevent things from happening too quickly. Our founding ancestors created a system to prevent things from happening absent extensive deliberation and agreement.

The good news is that it worked; the bad news is, also, that it worked. The worse news is that we have it today and it works for us, too—even when we do not want it to.

This means that we will have to compress decision-making time so we can move forward at the same pace as the world. This includes our members' worlds, and we need to be able to respond to the pace of their demands.

In traditional associations, the amount of time people are actually spending doing real work during that period that elapses between identifying a member opportunity or need and actually delivering the benefit is estimated to be about 10 to 15 percent. The remaining time tends to be consumed by "wait time." This is waiting for (1) the next group to meet to give permission to think further about what might done, in order to (2) propose something that will then be (3) recommended for budget approval, in order to be allowed to actually develop what will then be (4) re-authorized before implementation.

When we examine where "wait time" comes from in a traditional association model, we discover that, in the vast majority of cases, it comes from control needs that add no additional value to the decision. If we are to compress "wait time" to respond more quickly, we will have to replace unnecessary control with something else. The only set of conditions that can adequately and beneficially replace control is common information, clarity, and consensus on outcomes, trust, and the resources to do the work.

The implications for our decision processes are real. Our decision processes need to operate more quickly, be more maneuverable, and be outcome oriented.

Here is an illustration: Two years ago, the staff and elected leaders of an association approached its members saying several million dollars were needed to purchase and install a new computer system that would allow them to do their work more efficiently. After emitting a short, gasping sound, the members' answer was a resounding, "No!"

Two years later, the same staff and elected leadership once more approached the same membership. This time, however, it was after a long-range, strategic planning process that reached clarity and consensus on vision, mission, and goals describing how members' worlds would improve as a result of what the organization would do.

The leadership went to its members and said, "You have indicated to us that one of the goals you have is to have access to information and advice that you need to more effectively make business and professional decisions. We need to invest several million dollars over a period of five years to construct the systems and technology that will provide this for you and achieve your goal."

This time, the answer to the same proposal from the same group of people was "Yes!" There was still a bit of a gasping sound at the investment required, but the "yes" was unmistakable. This example shows that every decision we make must be driven and explained by the benefit that accrues to members as a result of implementation.

Sometimes association leaders get operationally insulated. While we get involved with our members, we must be equally involved in operational issues and not forget why we are trying to do something. It is not enough to focus simply on what we are proposing. This way, we often mistakenly assume members understand our intent. Members do not have access to the same stream of information leaders enjoy.

Market Sensitivity

Although association decision processes are becoming more market sensitive, this does not mean we take polls and surveys and make policy decisions based on their results. This is not the appropriate approach to association leadership. Market sensitivity means what we do for our members is motivated by anticipating what their needs will be. In the knowledge-based model, foresight about relevant future conditions of their world allows us to predict evolving needs, rather than just responding to current wants.

There is a logical protocol in being strategically thoughtful. First, identify what changes are occurring in our members' world. Based on that, anticipate what needs they will have. Based on that, determine what services the organization is well positioned to provide to meet those needs. Based on that, organize the association, its programs and its services in a way that expeditiously provides the activities meeting those evolving needs.

This is what is meant by market sensitivity; decisions balancing member wants and leadership's insights are knowledge based. Concern about the political correctness of the group making the decision is balanced by equal concern that the group has the necessary knowledge and expertise about what is being considered. It may not just agree to do something; it must agree to do the right thing. All this has extraordinary implications for us and the competencies we and our organizations will need as we enter the twenty-first century.

Preparedness

How prepared are we, and our organizations, to successfully sustain and execute the necessary combination of competencies required to succeed in the twenty-first century. Leaders of knowledge-based associations will master execution of competencies that may be divided into six clusters (Tecker and Fidler 1993):

1. possessing interpersonal skills,
2. valuing and using technology,
3. acquiring and using information,
4. understanding complex relationships,
5. deploying resources,
6. and exhibiting certain relevant personal characteristics.

Interpersonal skills relate to the need for executives to have the ability to work as members of groups, to teach others, to serve them, and to lead, negotiate, and work well with people from diverse cultural backgrounds. Leaders who are rigid, defensive, manipulating, controlling, and fearful will not be tolerated in the twenty-first century. Nor will leaders who are unwilling to take personal risks, who produce indirect communications, who cause fragmentation of groups, and who misunderstand the needs and intents of others.

This may be a dramatic shift in culture for some traditional associations. Leaders will be required who are able to integrate information, knowledge, capacity, psychological tools, and processes to effectively achieve clear, desired outcomes. Members will no longer tolerate a knee-jerk reactor, someone who does too little too late, or someone paralyzed by fear and immobilized by ego. While members may tolerate such undesirable qualities from their colleagues, they will not tolerate such attributes from association leaders.

Undesirable is someone who uses the past as the only indicator of the future. Also undesirable is someone who invests in equipment, but not in user training and upgrades or someone stingy who does not give people tools they need to accomplish their jobs.

Knowledge-based leaders will be required who possess the abilities to acquire and evaluate information, and who communicate it in ways that are relevant and understood. Members will not tolerate leaders who pursue their own visions and opinions regardless of data or member needs. They will not tolerate those who seek only information supporting their own visions or opinions or those who withhold information as a control tactic. They will not tolerate someone who is able to make a decision but is unable to communicate the rationale for making that decision.

Association leaders must remember that it is not merely their understanding of these characteristics that counts, it is their ability to actually conform to these needs and traits. All association leaders are perpetually sitting in "a fishbowl."

The twenty-first century will require leaders to be able to understand social, organizational, and technological systems. They will be able to evaluate and monitor progress, and be able to design "on the fly" new structures and innovative processes.

Individuals who look at each situation in a vacuum or who push on "X" and do not anticipate that "Y" will pop out will not be attractive. Someone who focuses only on fragments and details and who is not holistic or focused on outcomes, or someone who sees complexity but is immobilized will be undesirable.

The twenty-first century will require leaders who know how to prioritize and allocate time, money and material, space, and volunteer and staff resources. Those who waste energy and resources, who make much ado about nothing, and who generate lots of activity but no results will not be tolerated. Fragmentation of effort between organizations will not be tolerated where members' time and dollars are coming out of the same pocket, regardless of the political relationships between the organizations. Collaboration, not competition, will be a viable strategy for the twenty-first century.

Leaders will be required who possess the characteristics, attitudes, and perceptions bridging all the clusters of skills described earlier. Since the only thing that can be promised with any certainty about the future is that it will continue to be uncertain, managing through change will be the function of future leaders. They will do this much more easily in organizations that have committed to a knowledge-based operational model, philosophy, and culture.

Four "Service Niche" Templates for Associations

There are four basic, strategic models for knowledge-based associations. The first three models describe the nature of the relationship a member can expect to have with his or her association. The fourth model is peculiar to associations and relates more to reputation for executing a core function.

They are used to begin an association's dialogue about what core capabilities and organizational attributes will be most essential to its chosen future and culture. The model that will best earn the association a reputation for excellence should be selected. The models are:

1. Operational excellence
2. Product (program) leadership
3. Customer (member) intimacy
4. Representational effectiveness

Most knowledge-based associations will choose one of the models as a primary driver. Most associations will need to be somewhat competent at all four; however, only one of them must take precedence. This is because the organization is going to try to align all the parts of the organization—its resources, allocations, the kind of expertise attracted to it, the kind of work done, and the systems and processes employed—so they are targeted on achieving excellence in the positioning selected.

It is also necessary for associations successful in sustaining their activity to recognize that, occasionally, different business lines of the association require it to choose one or another of these models as the source of the reputation for excellence for that business line. The association, as an enterprise, however, must select one that it intends to be known for.

How is one of these models selected? Two things are taken into account. First, which of the four possibilities is most closely related to what members and prospective members would value the most?

Second, which of the four possibilities is most closely related to core capabilities that you possess or have a reasonable chance of accessing? In other words, which of the four is most closely aligned with what you know you are going to be able to do well?

In making a judgment about strategic positioning, an association would be in Utopia if it picked the model most related to what its members value and where it had the greatest competence. If that is Utopia, conversely, association Hell would be if leadership selected the model most valued by members, but where it had the least chance of ever creating the competencies needed to execute it well.

At that point, the choice might be to pick the second best model as a transitional strategy. This would allow the association to grow strength until it got to the point where it had the capacity to adopt the model of highest value to members. That stage would be bridged with a transition strategy.

Operational Excellence

The organization that selects this model delivers a combination of quality, price, and ease of purchase that no other organization in the market can match. This association is not a product or service innovator; being the first out with a new thing is not important. It does not cultivate one-on-one relationships with customers; it deals with masses, but it executes extraordinarily well. The commitment it makes is to guarantee value.

If that is what you are like, then, at a minimum, the four core capabilities required to execute this model are

1. cost efficiencies,
2. large volume for programs to reduce cost;
3. quality customer service;
4. rapid response of fulfillment capability;
5. and, probably most importantly, a number of other characteristics peculiar or unique to the association and its marketplace.

Product (Program) Leadership

An association whose primary business line is providing products and services to large volumes of people might find this second model an attractive selection. This model involves earning a reputation for being the source of leading-edge programs that expand the existing performance boundaries of the profession, constituency, or industry. Associations working with this model are sources of useful, new applications of existing programs, not breakthrough thinking, but innovation sufficient to capture attention.

These associations are committed to providing the best products and programs. The core competency required is a culture that values creativity. These associations have operational philosophies that include processes that support inventiveness and invention. An entrepreneurial culture is required that, more than anything, rewards and encourages risk.

If your organization operates with this model, you need a scanning mechanism to identify potential new programs before anybody else thinks of them. Product, programming, and leadership must really get out in front of the crest of the wave.

Program development capabilities and business and management processes must support program development engineered for speed. Leaders must be the first out with products and programs. If you are not the first out with them, you are not really leading, are you? You need a willingness to leapfrog your own latest program with something new. You need to be able to take leaps of faith into the next thing over the horizon. Associations with business lines of education and knowledge access will find this model an attractive option.

Customer or Member Intimacy

A third choice is built on customer or member intimacy. Here, bonds and relationships with members are built. The association does not deliver what the market wants, but what a specific customer wants. The association knows its members and customers and the products and services they each want and need. Constantly upgrading offerings, the organization stays one step ahead of its customers. Customer loyalty is cultivated as its greatest asset. Its commitment is, "We take care of you and your needs."

The core competencies of this model are relationship building and maintenance capabilities; relationship management; the ability to customize programs, services, and products; and the ability to focus on those that can be served best.

If your association operates with this model, it needs clarity in core membership and member databases that support customization of its programs. The association should be able to look at the behavioral track record of people who are taking advantage of what is offered. From that behavioral track record, you want to know who to tell when something new comes along, even before they know they might be interested in it.

A culture is needed that embraces deep and lasting relationships and provides specific rather than general responses. Authority should be delegated to those closest to the member or the customer, to those best able to understand and respond most quickly to what the member wants.

Representational Effectiveness

The fourth choice is representational effectiveness, where interests of an industry, profession, or interest area, can be advocated most successfully. Personalized relationships are maintained with powerful decision makers. Interests of the constituency represented are well positioned as being congruent with the public interest and political interests of decision makers. Organizations operating with this model require a sophisticated understanding of strategic position in the political marketplace.

If an opposing force is able to position what it is advocating as more in the public interest than what you are advocating, you lose. If an opposing force is able to position what you are advocating as being of greater, sometimes invisible, political interest to a public decision maker, you lose again. Strategic positions are being taken here.

The organization's effectiveness in representation must be recognized as a member benefit. The organization must be recognized as a source of valuable information to decision makers.

Organizations operating with knowledge-based philosophies have the ability to tie issues being advocated to the interests of the public and policy makers. They are able to frame their policy objectives in terms of "enlightened self interest:" that is, they emphasize benefit to the public as opposed to benefit to their constituency. They are also able to link their positions on issues to the political self interests of a policy maker.

Operating with this model requires anticipated knowledge of evolving issues so cases can be prepared before votes are required. Timely knowledge of the proposals, positions, opinions, and world views of others is needed, because the organization must understand the arguments against its position and where they are going to come from. This model works well to earn a reputation of excellence for trade associations that have advocacy as a primary business line.

Subtle, but Real Relationships

There are subtle but real relationships between some of these four choices. A trade association may select representational effectiveness as its first choice. If it is also able to achieve a good reputation and competencies in product and program leadership, that will support its representational effectiveness. In turn, its reputation as a source of leading-edge information will support its access to decision making if it is recognized as a source of thoughtful insight and up-to-date knowledge.

Choosing product and program leadership may be related to customer intimacy. If opportunities can be created for people to achieve a sense of community as they access the knowledge that you are giving them, you are going to get twice the benefit you expect.

Building a Sense of Community

During the next decade a very large proportion of associations' membership will still be from the "baby boom" generation. Two things are happening. This generation, which will continue to be a very large percent of their membership, is searching for a sense of community. Members of this generation are also looking for an opportunity to enjoy themselves.

The traditional communities in which people lived do not exist any more; people move too often. Ties to religious communities for that generation have never been that strong. So where are baby boomers looking?

Remember, this generation defines its members, in large measure, on the basis of what they do for a living. They draw a distinction between a career and a job. The confluence of these two phenomena, the search for community and the tendency to define your worth as a person on the basis of what you do for a living, places knowledge-based associations in a superb position as places to go for a feeling of community.

The second phenomenon related to this generation, which seeks enjoyment, comes from hints it takes from its subsequent generation of "baby busters." The knowledge-based association is not coldly data driven.

A review of the earlier discussion about generationally-related preferences is germane here. Remember, the past decade heard baby boomers saying, "I'm very busy. What I do is very important. Give me what I need. Give it to me quick. Tell me what to do. Give me the tools I need. Let me get out of there and get back to work." That was a decade where many of the social dimensions of programming were eliminated. Associations got rid of the reception and the banquet in favor of one more case study.

Now the reception and the banquet are back again, because that generation is borrowing some values from the later generation, which has always been amenable to socializing. It is not just making sure that there is time for the banquet at the annual convention, but that there is time for the open bar and dancing. That is not all—what is important is that every time or place where there is a memorable moment of membership and interaction needs to be fun.

Now more than ever, board meetings should be enjoyable. Serving on a committee is important, but being on a committee where it is fun to be involved is just as important. Going to an educational program is an opportunity to learn. It is also important for it to be an enjoyable experience.

If you do not position the organization to be a source of fun and a potential source of a sense of community, future generations of membership will surely go shopping for other places to go. The opportunity for enjoyable, personal interactions may prove to distinguish associations from on-line, interactive communities that may provide a sense of belonging but still tend to remain more impersonal over an extended period of time.

CHAPTER 9

Adopting a New Culture

Theory has been different than actual practice for many organizations operating with traditional approaches. Most associations began for the purpose of advocacy. Making policy was their purpose, so it is not surprising that, to be democratic in nature, a government-like model of decision making was adopted.

Eventually, though, many associations moved to providing services and products, not just advocacy, causing a dilemma. A political model of decision making, while well matched for advocacy, may not be well matched for making decisions about delivering products and services. If products and services are increasingly important to helping members achieve goals that have been established, there may be a significant mismatch in systems, processes, and culture.

Historic Approaches to Balance of Power

Since the 1980s, associations have discussed operational philosophy around issues related to the balance of power between staff and members. Association management students observed several distinct portraits of operational approaches, gave them labels, and tried to select which choice was the best "fit" for an association's mission, work plan, and culture. Each portrait had its own set of advantages and disadvantages, and certain aspects of the organization's structure and processes could be manipulated to achieve the right balance for each organization. All these traditional portraits, however, revolve around power distribution between groups, not around the distribution of knowledge among them.

Each of the portraits, listed in table 3, consists of three common parts: (1) who made the decisions, (2) based on what, and (3) in whose interest.

Over the last fifty years, many associations with the primary mission of advocating for their members' interests have operated with a "member responsive" philosophy. Associations with major focuses on providing products and services tended to function with a "product driven" orientation.

Organizations holding both advocacy and service as equally important missions tended to operate the public affairs side of the organization in a "member responsive" fashion. The service side of the organization employed a "product driven" approach. This dichotomy in organizational culture often created significant undercurrents of tension in resource allocation and work styles. Sometimes it divided the culture so

Table 3. Historic Approaches to Balance of Power in Associations

Staff Driven	• Staff makes decisions based on what the staff believes is best for the staff.
Staff Directed	• Staff makes decisions based on what the staff believes is best for the association.
Product Driven	• Staff makes decisions based on their perceptions of member needs and what existing or revised products would meet those needs at desired revenue levels.
Officer Driven	• The leadership oligarchy makes decisions based on what they believe is best for them.
Market Driven	• Member and staff leadership make decisions about what they think is best for the membership based on limited information about member wants. High-level strategy is often not reflected in program decisions or activity at the work level.
Member Responsive	• The leadership oligarchy makes decisions based on their perceptions of what members want and need.
Need Driven	• The leadership oligarchy makes decisions based on what they believe is best for the association.

severely that leadership allowed the organization to operate as market directed, while in reality the operation was "market driven," as defined in table 3.

In the "staff driven" philosophy, the staff makes decisions based on what it believes is best for the staff. At the other end of the spectrum is the "officer driven" philosophy. Here the leadership oligarchy makes decisions based on what they believe is best for them. The only difference between this operational philosophy and "staff driven" is who is serving their own self interest. From the point of view of the membership, the situation is the same.

Almost every association was conceived by a small group of people. The same people became the board, the staff, and the committee work force. They focused their attention on things that were in their own interest. Being "officer-driven" was not a problem at first. Problems occur when the membership expands. The program portfolio expands, but the operational philosophy does not change to keep pace.

The problem inherent in "staff directed" and "need driven" traditional operational philosophies is that decisions are being made on the basis of the interest of the association as a corporate enterprise. Decisions are not being made on the basis of what is best for the membership. Leaders of traditional associations easily fall into this trap because they spend so much time trying to maintain the efficacy of their operations. They sometimes forget why they are operating in the first place.

Here is a simple example. You have one dollar to spend. You have only two choices. You can either spend this dollar on a membership development campaign to increase the number of members and grow dues, or you can spend the dollar on improving the quality of an existing program for your current, core membership.

In "staff directed" and "need driven" operational philosophies, it would likely be spent on membership development because bigger is better, and it is in the best interest of the corporation to get bigger. This, however, may not be in the best interest of members. There is a difference.

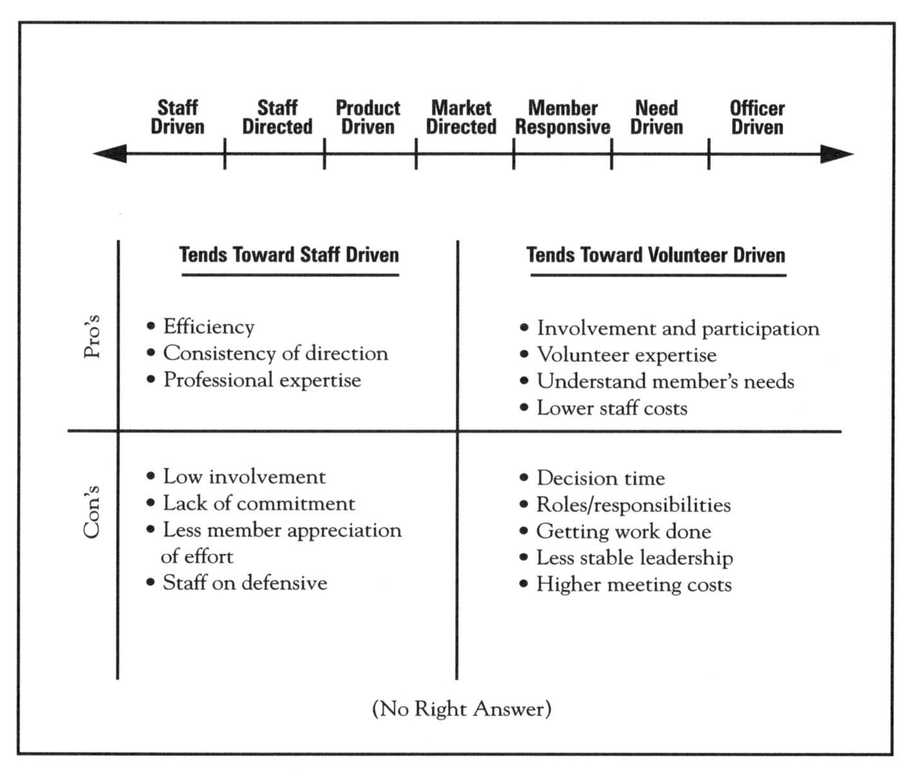

Figure 3. Balance of Power: A Continuum

For some time, it has been thought that associations should be "market driven," but close examination has revealed that this actually creates a multiple personality in many traditional associations. Cross-purposes, confusion, and duplication arises. Leadership is convinced it is doing certain kinds of work to move in certain directions and carefully documents this in a spiral-bound, glossy-covered document called the long-range, strategic plan. When you look, though, at what staff actually does and what the committees are actually working on, the two agendas have little or no relationship to each other.

Regardless of the specifics of the philosophy, these historic choices have all been driven by concern over the distribution of power. For that reason, none of them are likely to be sufficiently attractive to tomorrow's members.

Make Way for a More Informed Approach

Knowledge-based decision making is very different from conventional operational philosophies because its driver is different. It is not driven by concern about the distribution of power. In a knowledge-based enterprise, the value placed on expertise and insight creates a powerful consultative relationship between staff and members engaged in decision making and working together. The political model of operation and culture is supplanted by a more informed approach that maintains the appropriate balance of power while increasing the effectiveness of an enterprise focused on important outcomes.

Foundations in Place

The foundations for many of the systems required to make a knowledge-based operational philosophy real are already in place in many associations. Most associations, however, will need to significantly alter the behavior of their member and staff decision makers and work forces to make the philosophy more than just a subject of discussion, promise, and conjecture.

Association leaders exposed to the concept of a knowledge-based enterprise express virtually universal need to move toward such decision-making capabilities as quickly as possible. However, while some associations exhibit one or another of the characteristics of knowledge-based enterprises, we are not aware of any association that has successfully integrated and sustained all the fundamentals. Even the most competent associations express the belief that they have much to learn before achieving a degree of decision-making maturity they would consider sufficient for the demands of the next century.

Several factors are likely to heavily influence associations' knowledge bases, information exchange systems, decision-making approaches, directions, structures, systems and processes, cultures, and strategies:

- the more things are expected to change the more they will need to operate with increased awareness;
- data bases will not be substitutes for "informed intuition," they will both enable and demand it;
- successful leadership will be exercised with informed intuition.

Characteristics of the New Association

How can an association with a knowledge-based operational philosophy maintain an environment conducive to "informed intuition?" How will its approach be different than the historical approaches of many associations? It will be remarkably different in at least three related ways.

1. The twentieth-century paradigm of information as power will be different—in reality, not just in romanticized leadership claims about their organization. Information will produce power when it is distributed, accessed, and intelligently used for actual decision making. It will not produce power for the individual or group who has it and holds it for some anticipated political advantage or leverage at a later date. In fact, increasingly, such behavior is likely to be ostracized within and among organizations.
2. Decision making at all levels will be better informed by easier access to useful information. People in the association accountable for results will really have the authority to make decisions and act in a fashion necessary to accomplish their responsibilities.
3. Traditional concern for the protocol of who exercises what powers in an association will be superseded by concern about effectiveness. Power will be executed by people properly knowledgeable about issues and well positioned to act effectively. Real behavioral change, not just change in the policy and procedures manual, will be the norm. In other words, the cultures of successful associations will be different.

Gearing Up for Tomorrow

What will successful associations need to be able to do in a world where:

- Business and personal needs of key member segments are changing rapidly

- A constantly evolving balance between customized responsiveness to an individual member's expectations *and* the desire for a sense of common community are competitive advantages
- There are many ways for members to meet needs associations have traditionally served

A New Dynamic

Conventional wisdom holds that the decision to join an association is made on the basis of the match between a prospective member's highest-priority needs and the programs offered by the association. Historically, this has been the determining factor, especially for trade and professional associations and societies. When an association wanted to keep or grow membership, it would adjust its services and their promotion. Recent research, however, strongly suggests this will be insufficient as we move into the next century.

As mentioned earlier, tomorrow's members are as concerned with the projected image of an association as they are with the benefit package it offers. This is increasingly playing a parallel and almost equal role in the decision to join or renew. Members will be increasingly interested in identity and values. Would they be proud to affiliate with the attributes and traits of the association, as they perceive them? This is what association professionals refer to as the "culture" of the organization. Where the match is a bad one, other places—some real, some virtual—will be chosen as answers to an individual's needs.

This is something many philanthropic organizations already struggle with daily; it appears to be particularly important to younger members and prospects. The association that remains insensitive to this dynamic runs the risk of not surviving past the year 2000.

For associations with primary business lines of information and education, this will pose a particularly difficult challenge. As more alternative, often electronic, sources of interpreted data and learning opportunities develop, these associations will have to differentiate themselves as attractive investments in increasingly innovative ways. Marketing and technology will be essential, core competencies of the successful association for at least the next twenty years, but alone they will not be enough.

Desire for Community

Today's thirty year old who will be active in an association for another fifty years—commonly expresses a powerful need for "community." (Many observers of today's preteens—the ten year olds who will be at the prime association age of thirty plus over the next twenty years—indicate this value is equally strong in this group.)

The very nature of the association experience will need to be attractive if an association is to successfully compete with a larger variety of places where discretionary time can be invested. Active involvement has always needed to be an enjoyable experience; but, for the next seventy-five years, the character of organizations that people will find enjoyable will be changing (see table 4). The particular attributes of this change will differ markedly from one successful organization to the next—there is no one best way to do it. The generic directions, however, are definable. Many of those associations that will succeed in the next century are already working toward them today.

Table 4. Ways Associations Will Need to React to Tomorrow's Environment

In a World Where:	Associations Will Need To:
• Business needs of at least some member segments are changing rapidly • Structure or nature of the industry/profession is undergoing significant changes • Responsiveness to member needs is a significant competitive advantage over other organizations • Member needs assessment data indicates the association has not been responsive in the past	• Be able to create new products or services swiftly in response to fast-developing and changing markets, needs, or opportunities
• Members experiment constantly, move fast, see if an idea works, and if it doesn't, move on to the next	• Be able to also work this way; since their members will expect similar capabilities in their association
• Business lines, not just products and services, change frequently • Functions or relationships among functions required to design, develop, and/or deliver products and services change in response to market changes	• Be able to change organizational structures in response to market changes • Be able to use self-managed teams, where all members have the same information, and lots of it; to share information broadly among all who have an interest (financial information, needs assessment, etc.) in a process of decision making and consensus building
• Key expertise is not available in the organization's work force (staff or volunteers) • Essential functions or skills are required for specific events or activities, but not required on a continual or even basis	• Be able to deal with anyone necessary to get the job done, using modular structures where appropriate

CHAPTER 10

Strategic Planning and Shared Accountability

Volumes have been written on strategic planning and strategy. It is not our intent to rewrite or summarize them here. There are some perspectives about strategy planning, however, that are especially germane in a knowledge-based association. First, let us examine some of the very basic assumptions about using a strategic approach to planning in an association environment.

It is important to recognize that strategic planning and long-range planning are not the same thing. The terms are often interchanged mistakenly. Long-range planning refers to the period of time for which the plan is offered. Strategic planning refers to the particular approach to planning employed.

The knowledge-based association views strategic planning as a process rather than a project or product. This shift in paradigm is reflected in changes in language now used to refer to the identification of strategy. The term "strategic planning" is increasingly being replaced by purposeful reference to a process of planning that is strategic.

Clear Direction

Establishing a clear direction is a fundamental responsibility of the leadership team of any organization. This is established when the leadership team comes to consensus on answers to two questions. First, where is this organization going? Second, why is it going there: what is its purpose and reason for existence? Unfortunately, the answers are often misstated.

Direction should result from the leadership team envisioning the future, putting the headlights on high beams, and announcing where they would like the organization to be at some point out there in time. It is best when direction is articulated in some type of strategic plan that focuses on outcomes. Strategic direction and strategic plans need to focus on outcomes.

What members really care about is that there is some kind of plan in place to help build perceivable benefits. What is coming out of the end of the pipe for them? They expect the leadership team to have the right planning and processes in place to deliver these.

There is nothing magical about strategic plans. There have been many organizations, both for profit and not for profit, that had leadership teams that came to consensus on direction and, although the answers to those two important questions were never articulated in a strategic plan, were very successful. Conversely, there are a number of organizations with strategic plans that sit in binders on shelves and are never used by leadership teams, and they are not successful.

Strategic planning is not an end-all or a be-all. Its not anything, actually, until the leadership team uses it to make something happen.

How Do Organizations Use Strategic Plans?

There is a fair amount of confusion and mixed opinion about what is truly a long-range, strategic plan. The viable lifetime of a strategic plan needs to be determined by each association based on the pace of change in its relevant environment. It is generally critical that the process for planning strategically routinely involve periodic review and update based on new information and past experience.

Either the board or some other segment of leadership needs to formally update the plan annually and be prepared to alter it routinely in response to new opportunities and challenges. While the strategic direction reflected in vision, mission, and goals usually remains viable for the life of a plan, responsive associations will alter or abandon strategy and activity as new realities require.

When Is a Plan Really Strategic?

What makes a plan strategic is that it asks what the organization is not doing today that it had better be doing well in the future to reach its objectives. It implies change. It implies doing less of something the organization does today, doing something totally new, or deleting something being done today. A truly strategic plan emerges from a process that carefully considers the strategic intent of the organization. It:

- Emphasizes the resourcefulness of the organization more than the resources it currently controls
- Establishes goals that exceed the present grasp and existing resources of the organization
- Motivates the organization to close the gap between what is and what leadership wants it to be by setting challenges that focus efforts on the near to medium term
- Does not include an operational component (this makes the plan much simpler)

When doing strategic analysis, we look at present and future dimensions. Associations should not simply look at the here and now or look only into the future. The present and the future should be analyzed simultaneously.

Strategic analysis requires internal and external examination. What is going on within the association, and what is going on in the larger environment outside? How does it focus on the big issues?

Five Characteristics of Strategic Planning

Effective long-range planning that is strategic involves a process where (1) the process itself is as important as its products; (2) the process is highly participative; (3) all interested parties participate in the process as partners; (4) the products of the planning process (reports and documents) are clear, concise, and easy to understand; and (5) the long-range planning process is linked to annual planning, budgeting, and evaluation.

There are ways of constructing the planning process, where consensus moves the group forward, never using the dangerously simple "one more than 50 percent" rule to make a decision. It is important to remember, however, that decisions represent priorities to be implemented.

Impact, Consequence, and Immediacy

Delineating priorities is best done by sharing and understanding, at the outset, a common set of principles defining what a priority is. Three factors most useful to associations and necessary to take into account when planning and establishing priorities are impact, consequence, and immediacy.

- *Impact* is the measure of strategic importance that deals with relationships. How many other things are related to that priority issue? How many other things depend on it?
- *Consequence* is the measure of strategic importance that relates to intensity. How much bad or how much good will it do for us?
- *Immediacy* is a measure of strategic importance that has to do with time. It is, literally, our window in time; how much time do we have to get it done?

When a group is able to agree on the criteria it will use to determine what its strategic priorities are, there is a much higher probability of consensus among staff and board. One reason a vote on priorities may not be a good idea is that voting has a tendency to result in a commitment to a level of decision making that the planning process is not really ready for.

Once strategic issues are identified, it is still necessary to study them before crafting critical objectives to respond to them. A plan should not be built based on perceptual assumptions that may not, in fact, be correct.

Importance of Differing Perceptions

Staff and elected leadership in a knowledge-based environment should be encouraged to have different perceptions. That is one of the practical values of bringing them together as partners, and it is the third of the five characteristics of strategic planning. Staff, because of the nature of its duties, spends much more time in an information stream related to issues significant to the association's mission than any elected officer. Staff is in that stream deeper and longer. People's perceptions of what is important are, of course, based on the information they have available. The information stream that staff has available is broader, deeper, and considerably different from most of the information elected officers have available.

In a knowledge-based operation, it is very wise and extremely helpful for staff to try, for a given period of time before the planning session, to increase the confluence between the information stream that the officers have and the one they have. This will not guarantee that there still will not be different opinions; in fact, differing opinions are desirable. It is the confluence of the differing perceptions that increases the probability that judgments ultimately made will, in fact, be good for the association.

In a knowledge-based operation, it is vital that the officers be sensitive to the fact that their perceptions of what is important will differ from the perceptions of the vast majority of members. This is because, by virtue of their participation in the association as officers, their information stream differs from that of the members.

Planning as a Process

Because of rapid change in the environment and in information streams, it is more vital than ever that we understand that planning in an association is a process. It is not an isolated event. Status reports related to planning are the middle of something, not the end. The planning process, in a knowledge-based organization, if done properly, is a commitment to a way of collecting information and using it to make decisions about where the association is heading. It is done in a formative fashion that allows the course to be adjusted along the way.

Needs Assessment Strategy

There is an infrastructure that must be in place for planning to result in effective implementation. One of the pieces of that infrastructure is a needs assessment strategy. This is a deliberate, continuous process—a planned series of techniques or events designed to let leaders continually assess information from members about their needs, problems, and expectations. Continuous dipping of the bucket in that moving information stream allows leadership to jump ahead to implement whatever plan emerges from the planning process.

The object of a plan is to achieve what is important, not just to follow the plan. If the plan must be changed, it should be. A needs assessment strategy increases the probability that staff and board will share a common base of information about members' perceptions of needs, challenges, and problems. It is another strategy that can be used to bring staff and board closer together. It is a great bridge for the third characteristic of effective strategic planning (all interested parties participate in the process as partners).

Equal-Partner Participation in Developing Strategy

In an environment with a knowledge-based philosophy, all parties participate in planning as equal partners: elected officers, leaders of committees, senior staff members, perhaps even other key players of organizations outside the association who have some interest in what the association is involved in. Academics and members of regulatory agencies are examples. A substantial list of such individuals who are germane to a particular association could be built very easily.

When these people gather around the table to plan, there is no hierarchy. This reflects a committed recognition that judgments made with any degree of certainty can evolve only from this diversity of interests, perceptions, experiences, and expertise.

Theoretically, from these different perspectives, something will emerge that represents common self interest. There is a much greater probability that what emerges will be important and beneficial to all rather than something identified, with no test or challenge, by a single individual thinking alone in a room somewhere.

Please do not misunderstand this concept. Planning is done among equal partners. The results of the planning process are then fit into the normal governance process of the association. The board has the ethical, legal, and fiduciary responsibility to say "yea" or "nay" to whatever may have evolved from that planning activity. The governance hierarchy operates from the plan once constructed, but while the plan is growing, all participants are equal partners.

Something else exists in that dynamic that later has a huge payoff for the organization. Because the board has already been actively participating in developing what it will later review for the purposes of approval, the probability of approval is dramatically increased. In a knowledge-based association body, other than the board of directors, a planning committee can operate with specific responsibility to devise and guide the planning process or even to engage in some of the fine-tuning of things between major planning events.

Understanding and Commitment

It is crucial for at least a critical mass of the governing board to actively participate in the planning process. If they do not, they will have no understanding of where the plan came from. They will have little or no commitment to the plan. In fact they often will see themselves as outside judges, and they will be looking for ways to critique or find fault.

In an association, because of its voluntary nature, two things have to be in place for a plan to be implemented. First, the people who will have to implement the plan have to understand it. How can one implement something one does not understand? Second, the people who will have to implement the plan must be committed to it. Why would anyone bother to implement something for which one feels no sense of ownership?

Relevant to these points is the fact that there are two primary implementers of plans in associations. One operates on the policy level—the board. The other is the senior staff, usually charged with implementation. There is only one way to create understanding and commitment between the two, and that is through meaningful, mutual involvement. Absent understanding, the two parties to implementation cannot make it happen. Absent commitment, they will not bother to.

In a knowledge-based association, the board's active participation in the planning process as an equal partner has additional payoffs. At those monthly or quarterly board meetings, they have actively participated in developing strategy in the environmental scanning processes and in selecting critical objectives from an almost endless list. As a result, the board, as a body, is better positioned to make decisions on routine matters. It is influenced by the larger picture its members have created for themselves. So even routine decisions are enhanced by virtue of the board's participation as a partner.

Two conditions tend to predict where strategic planning will not work. First, in those places where the strategic planning is successful, the people who have to do the implementing are active participants in the planning. In places where it does not work, one group does the planning, and another group is expected to carry out the plan—but with no participation in the planning.

The second thing that makes a difference is that the long-range strategic plan is linked to annual planning, budgeting, and evaluation to create a formative management and evaluation system. In some associations it is called a management accountability program. Whatever its label, it is a systematic approach that enables long-range strategy and judgments about what must be done each year. It is also a way of assessing the plan and the progress being made even while it is happening.

Formative Versus Summative Planning

The terms "formative" and "summative" have specific meanings in a knowledge-based association. Summative planning, management, and evaluation are what most associations have traditionally done. Summative stems from the word "sum" or "summary." Again, in summative planning, management, and evaluation, something is examined after it is over, and decisions are then made as to whether it is satisfactory or not. We are literally looking at the past and then making a judgment about whether we accomplished what we set out to do.

Formative stems from the root "to form" or "to shape." As discussed earlier, in formative planning, management, and evaluation, we look at things while they are unfolding to see whether we are headed where we wanted to go. This way we can adjust our course along the way if necessary.

Remember the earlier referenced airline pilot analogy. If you are an airline pilot, summative evaluation of your landing does you very little good. It is not very helpful, after landing, to discover that you have missed the runway. On the other hand, formal, formative appraisal of your landing is very helpful. It tells you, while you are approaching landing, whether you are too high, too low, too far to the left, or too far to the right, so you can adjust your course as needed.

Understandable Plans

Another important characteristic of successful planning is that its products must be clear, concise, and easy to understand. Plans that are heavily weighted with statistical analysis may be impressive, but the tendency is not to use them. The more concise and precise the articulation of direction can be, the more useful it will be. Basic logic indicates that it is highly unlikely that people will follow a plan they cannot understand.

The readability of planning documents must reasonably match members' sophistication. Use analogies and language with which members are comfortable and that they can relate to in what they normally do in their own businesses, enterprises, and environments. This creates a comfort level that has as much to do with acceptance of the plan as does its actual substance and content. This is not a suggestion to be manipulative. It is a suggestion that leaders be good communicators and pay as much attention to whether the message they want to send is being correctly received as they pay to sending the message.

Periodic Review of the Plan

Each year should begin with a strategic planning process that first examines the long-range plan created two or three years ago. The association determines whether it can say it is still valid now. Then it takes a second look at things occurring in the environment that are currently affecting association members. Finally, it looks at things inside the association. It creates a list of strategic issues, in terms of strengths and weaknesses, to be addressed by a partnership of board and staff. This process will be of practical benefit to staff-board relationships throughout the rest of that year. The kind of outcome-focused partnership that exists in a knowledge-based organization is re-established at the beginning of each year.

By virtue of participation of the partners, the board and staff are able to "get into each other's heads" a little bit. Staff, when it comes time to implement, has a much better idea of what the board really wants because they sat around the table, too, during deliberations. When staff takes an action it is able to say to the board, "Listen, remember when we said we wanted to do this; now here's how this fits into that picture we created," and the board will understand.

Every year, organizations should not re-do their entire long-range plans. Plans are set for a five- or ten-year period, and they are fine-tuned each year along the way. In effective associations there is a major, strategic, long-range planning activity about every four years because, about every four years, two things have occurred. One is that the variables of the environment have changed dramatically. The other is that probably over 50 percent of the leadership has changed by that time.

This means that some people now in leadership positions have no memory of how or why the association decided that what is in the current plan is appropriate for the association, and they have no sense of ownership. So it is time to revisit, analyze, and establish ownership once more. Again, this makes planning in a knowledge-based organization a commitment to a process, not an event or isolated occurrence.

Because of this leadership turnover, in a knowledge-based environment, it is important to conduct a participatory, long-range, strategic planning activity, at a minimum of about every four years. If the system is set right initially, each year the long-range view will be again examined, but time will be spent attending to strategies and critical objectives for the coming year. Strategy and activity is adjusted each year of the plan while preserving basic direction. Assuming no cataclysmic event occurs in the association environment, the knowledge-based association is able to balance a coherent direction over time with easy flexibility.

Leading the Planning Process

It is not wise to permit any individual who might be perceived as having a vested interest in the direction of the association to serve as a leader to the planning process. To avoid that, there are a few choices. One is that an outside facilitator can be hired. The second is that a colleague from another organization can be sought to serve as a facilitator for the planning session. It is important to avoid any perception that the facilitator of the process has a vested interest in the substantive decisions that will be made.

Some associations have operated with a brick wall between the roles of the chief staff officer and the board, separating them almost completely. One side of the brick wall says "policy prerogative" and the other side says "administration or management." As a result, many associations spend more time arguing over who should make what decision than they spend making actual decisions.

In the twenty-first century, boards and senior staff, represented by the chief staff officer, will work together in this consultative partnership, each to represent a major aspect of the association's functioning. They may represent setting policy, administering, deciding what to do, or deciding how to do it. Most likely, both senior staff and board, and certainly the executive committee, will each be involved in every aspect of the association's operation. Twenty-first century technology will allow direct involvement of individual members in on-line conversations about major issues of strategic direction or policy. However, understanding between the board and senior staff about who will be involved in which of these association matters and who will have the final decision authority will be crucially important.

Table 5. Differences Between Governance and Management

Governance	Management
• Specifies outcomes, constraints, and desires.	• Specifies process to achieve outcomes within governance constraints.
• May suggest how best to accomplish desired outcomes.	• Must participate in decisions about constraints to ensure flexibility required to accomplish outcomes.
• Determines financial resources available to management and generally where the available resources are to be allocated.	• Informs governance of resources required and recommends cost-effective allocation.
• Identifies information required to make sound policy decisions and makes decisions regarding policy.	• Identifies information needed for sound policy decision making; may make policy deliberations. Specifies process for carrying out policy.
• Maintains focus on the good of the organization.	• Maintains focus on the good of the organization.
• Monitors progress and initiates conflict resolution where required to move the association ahead.	• Monitors progress and initiates conflict resolution where required to move the association ahead.

A Common Information Stream

A knowledge-based environment produces an almost common information stream between the board and the staff that is focused on the best interests of members. Board and staff need to be sitting around a table together and thinking about the future as equal partners.

Note what is happening here. No discussion of power or authority takes place. What is coming around the bend is being discussed. What do staff and board, together, see as important to the association? No necessity is created for the board members to defend their policy prerogatives.

Support Systems for Strategic Planning

Certain systems are required to support good, strategic planning. One that has already been mentioned is the needs assessment strategy. That is the carefully planned series of events, pre-budgeted to continuously occur, that allows collection of information directly from membership relating to problems they are and/or will be facing. These could include challenges and opportunities that they see around the corner, satisfaction or dissatisfaction with current association activities, and other information. Sometimes these activities might include bouncing a proposed association activity off the group before it is developed and executed.

The needs assessment strategy is just that—a strategy. It is not a single survey or a single event; it is a series of activities. It could include focus group activity, a discussion group using advisory committees, or doing telephone interviewing or consultation with targeted groups of key people in the association. Precisely which kind of needs assessment activity used is entirely up to you. But, in a knowledge-based association, having access to incoming, evolving information is critical to an effective, strategic planning process that is adjustable.

Policies

Another critical system is the policy system, which has two basic parts. One is a formal manual that records the decisions the board makes about policy matters so already-decided problems are not re-discussed. That manual has an internal portion, policies that deal with the association as an enterprise, and an external portion, positions that have been taken on issues.

A policy manual maintained by staff is critical for managing the information exchange with a board whose membership changes over time. In a knowledge-based association, the policy manual helps create institutional memory. This provides balance between past practice and innovation and between wasting time redoing and using time to rethink.

The second part of the policy system relates to its use as an operational technique that precludes the board from making a decision the very first time it talks about something important, absent information from staff, a committee, or its own unpressured, crystallized thinking. The major planning mistakes made in associations that are not knowledge based are changes to well-thought-out plans that occur when boards "shoot from the hip" because they do not have the proper insight.

Proper policy development should call for (1) identifying the problem, issue, or need; (2) researching by either committee or staff; (3) presenting information along with alternatives and the advantages and disadvantages of each alternative; and, finally, (4) making a recommendation.

Organizing the Board's Information Stream

It is important to manage the information stream that comes to the board, either in a notebook or in an electronic format. A style of organization that is particularly effective for knowledge-based associations is a loose-leaf notebook, or electronic notebook image in a laptop, that has a series of tabs with pages behind each tab. After the last tab in this notebook are some things that never come out. These might include bylaws, budget, an organization chart, and the strategic, long-range plan. These are the kinds of things board members always want and need to refer to.

Each of the other tabs is numbered, with each number standing for an item on the agenda. Behind each of those tabs is a page that looks like this:

1. The top of the page says "Agenda Item." It has a number and a name.
2. Underneath it there are two boxes: one labeled "For Information," the other labeled "For Action." The box the board is being asked to work on is checked so that the board members know exactly what is facing them.
3. Underneath this is a little section that says "Background." Here, in no more than a paragraph or two, is a discussion about what this item means and why it is on the agenda.
4. Beneath "Background" is a section titled "Existing Policy." There, the board is informed of policies that currently exist in the policy manual that are relevant to the issue before them. If there are no existing policies on the matter at hand, then past practices are discussed so precedents might be followed.
5. The next section is headed simply, "Discussion." Here, in several paragraphs if necessary, the staff or a committee, whoever is offering this cover page, will state the relevant information about the issue that relates to the four essential questions of a knowledge-based decision. This may include pro's and con's, advantages and disadvantages, alternative approaches, attendant consequences, whatever the board should be aware of in making the decision.
6. The last section is "Recommendations." This section should contain recommendations to the board for actions on which they can vote "yes" or "no." Boards cannot vote anything other than a "yes" or a "no." If they do not like the choices, then they use parliamentary procedure to amend the resolution until it gets to the point where they can vote "yes" or "no." If they are not voting "yes" or "no," they are planning or designing, not setting policy.

In effective associations, where the planning process is as described, recommendations tend to come to the board jointly from the chief staff officer and the executive committee.

Again, in a knowledge-based association, a plan that is strategic involves an evolving document. To really understand what makes it effective, attention must be paid to the things that help manage the information stream between staff, member-decision makers, and implementers as that plan is developed and executed.

Developing a Shared Accountability Program

In a knowledge-based environment, these procedures can work particularly well when combined with "a shared accountability program." As a result of the planning process, critical objectives for a specified time period are identified. This is not a managing-by-objectives system requiring an objective to be developed for everything. In successful associations and partnerships that effectively and collaboratively execute plans that achieve important things, there is always clear articulation of what the priorities are.

Here is a quick self-test. If you were asked to state the five or ten most important things for your association to accomplish during the next two to three years, could you do it? If you were asked to show where, in writing, those items were listed, could you find the document? If your board members were asked the same questions, would they give the same answers? If your members or staff were asked the same questions, would they give the same answers? What a shared accountability program does, as a management planning and control process, is create an opportunity for the leadership partnership, the board and staff functioning together, to track and demonstrate actual achievement of important things.

Here are the steps. Out of the planning process emerges a series of critical objectives—not everything, but the most important things to accomplish each year for the entire, three- to five-year plan. For each critical objective, an action plan is developed. The action plan is not a voluminous document; it is simply three columns.

1. The first column is headed "Key Events." In this column go the five or ten important activities that must be accomplished to move the association from where it is now to where it said it wanted to go. If there are less than five events, this needs to be thought about more carefully. Something was probably missed. If there are more than ten events, planners may have bitten off more than somebody else can chew.
2. The second column is headed "Responsibilities." In this column goes the name of the person or position responsible for each event. The name of a group never goes in that column because groups can't be accountable for anything. If a group is involved, put the name of a person there and put the name of the group in parentheses.
3. The last column is "Target Dates." In this column are identified dates by which each of those key events needs to be accomplished.

Indicators of Achievement

At the same time critical objectives are agreed on, "indicators of achievement" are developed. The indicators of achievement are three or four sentences, standards, that describe what the board and staff will use to judge whether, and to what extent, the critical objective was actually accomplished. Those indicators of achievement are developed at the same time critical objectives are set, not afterwards.

There is an important, practical value to this exercise. As the executive committee and chief executive work out the indicators of achievement, they come to a mutual understanding of what is truly meant by the objective. Later, no one will say, "I did achieve it," with someone else saying, "Well, but you really didn't."

Some of these target dates can also be used to develop a budget or establish estimated resources required for each critical objective. What will be required in people power? What equipment will this require? What money? What fees, etc.? Standard budgeting formats can be used to do this; new line items don't need to be invented.

When the estimated resources that will be required are considered, however, some of these target dates become more important than others because they represent dates for key events critical to executing strategy and achieving the objective. They may be called "milestones." Using milestones makes this planning process formative and sensitive to the five characteristics of effective planning.

Reporting on Progress

Some knowledge-based associations are embedding in their board meeting agendas a new item between Old Business and New Business called "Accountability Program," "Strategic Plan Report," or some other name with which they are comfortable. Before the board meeting, the chief executive officer prepares and sends to the board a brief progress report on the critical objectives.

This report simply shows "progress, problems, and next steps," and gives a little information about each critical objective. This allows the board of a knowledge-based association to focus its attention on issues of strategic direction and policy, not operations or administration.

Here is a sample scenario: At the board meeting, the chief staff executive might say to the board, "Ladies and gentlemen of the board, you'll recall that, as a result of our strategic and annual planning process, we said that, at this point in time, we'd like to have key event number three accomplished. This is our critical objective related to implementing a new, computer-assisted, virtual work group system. I'm pleased to report that, not only have we accomplished agenda item number three before schedule, but it looks like we're going to get the whole thing done sooner than we expected and for less money than we thought." (The board members will probably cheer.)

Or, the chief staff officer may come to the board and say "Ladies and gentlemen of the board, you will recall that we had hoped, by this point in time, to have accomplished event number four, critical objective number three. Unfortunately, I have to report that we have been unable to bring together the three committees that must meet to develop specifications." In such event, you now have a choice. You could say to the board "Well, what do you want to do?" Or you could say, instead, to the board, "Staff has looked at this," or "The XYZ committee has thought about it, and we see the following as alternatives and recommend X." The board may not cheer, but it has something constructive and progressive to think about.

In this case, it is time to examine the alternatives. Should the objective be changed? Maybe the organization bit off more than it could chew. Should the key events be changed? You can get there, but you will have to do it differently. Should the target date be extended? You can do it, but it is going to take longer. Or, is it necessary to pump in more resources?

Observe what has happened here. The planning process has been used to create shared accountability between board and senior staff. They operate together, as partners; the participatory, strategic planning approach is used, a structured process for board and staff to identify things they see are most important to achieve. An information stream is maintained between the key players that allows them, together, to keep track of progress and to make adjustments, so that later they do not discover that they did not achieve what they set out to do. Accountability is used to manage strategically, rather than merely holding management accountable for the success of strategy.

Responding Versus Reacting

Strategy is defined here as an organized response to the environment. Note the term used here is "response" not "reaction." Organizations that do not plan strategically, react. Organizations that plan longer term and strategically, respond. This approach to planning helps us position ourselves for a desired future rather than drift until we find ourselves reacting to a future someone else created.

Response to the environment refers to that critical element of strategic planning where organizations look at and react to the world in which we are functioning.

Strategic planning differs from traditional planning in that it is not simply a process of creating a "wish list" or delineating ideas that seem best at the moment. Strategic planning allows associations to look at reality, build alternatives, select from those alternatives, and increase the probability that they will end up where they want to be based on a particular set of goals.

This all must begin, however, with a clear declaration or description of where it is we are trying to go. If a plan does not include goals describing the condition or attribute an organization seeks to achieve, then it is not strategic. In the past, plans were often built that were long lists of options that people could take, but without any description of what was supposed to happen when all those options were taken.

Four Basic Variables of Planning

Every organization has to address the specifics of the strategic planning approach that will have the greatest meaning for it. Four variables will need to be balanced.

1. Cost: how much money needs to be invested?
2. Participation: how many people, and which people, need to be actively involved in the process?
3. Certainty: how certain do you want to be about the judgments made in the planning process and about the information used to make those judgments?
4. Time: how much time do you have to spend on the planning process, initially and over time, to maintain it? Whose time do you have to invest?

Every organization, and especially small- and medium-sized enterprises, will need to find an appropriate balance among these four variables. This constitutes "the plan for planning."

Certainty refers to two things. First, to what extent do you want to be sure the information you are using to make your judgments is solid, accurate, and defensible? Second, to what extent do you want to be sure that the judgments you are making are right? In a knowledge-based approach to strategic planning, certainty refers a level of comfort in decision-making. Usually, the more sources of information we have, and the greater the number of ways by which we collect it, the more certain we will be about the defensibility of that information. Cost and time can increase here, but the trade off is the degree of confidence we have in our decisions.

Usually, the more people involved in decision making, and the greater the number of times we go over what we think our information is telling us, the greater is our certainty about the quality of the judgments we are making. In a knowledge-based organization, planning is almost always strategic and occurs constantly. With this approach, therefore, there is a natural increase in the level of confidence we have in all of our decisions over time.

Build on Strengths

In a practical approach to long-range planning, strengths are built on and weaknesses are strengthened. Where necessary to achieve a critical outcome, as much attention is paid to what we do well as to what we need to improve on and what needs must be filled.

Fundamentally, most associations are usually better off building on things they already do well, rather than trying to do new things they have never done before or expanding into new businesses where they have no prior experience. Current, strong positions must be carefully identified to build on them. Not only is this efficient, but the probability of success is high.

Weaknesses must be attended to honestly, carefully, without rancor, and without self-punishment or deprecation. Honestly, what is it that we do not do so well? Often, we find, what we need to improve on has as much to do with what is going on around us as it has to do with personal things about us. Frequently, in a strategic, long-range planning process in an association, leaders get confused and think failure to be able take advantage of conditions in the environment is a condemnation of their personal talents, strength, or competence.

More often, it simply reflects a mismatch between what we do well and what that specific aspect of the environment requires us to do. That particular mistake is often made when we try to be something we are not, rather than trying to build on what we truly are. In a knowledge-based approach, careful consideration of our capacity and strategic position allows us to define a service niche that reflects high value to members and the potential for excellence.

In the twenty-first century, successful organizations will view the process of planning strategically as an investment, not as a cost. We must understand our world and that of our customers before we can turn our attention to optimizing our organization as an enterprise. We will need to look at our program of work and our portfolio of products and services. Our current and/or developing portfolio of products and/or services must be examined to ensure it is properly matched to where we see ourselves headed in the future. Do we currently have in place those things that will satisfy the wants and needs of today's and tomorrow's members and customers?

Anticipating Future Needs

If, in our program portfolio, we do not have in place lines of business, products, or approaches to service that will meet future needs of our member/customer base, and if there exits a larger group that would benefit from what we currently offer, should we change our base? Or, should we begin to expand our products and services, refine them, or recondition them so we can better match what we currently offer to our present customer base? Or, do we need to plan creation of new products and services for our portfolio to meet tomorrow's needs?

Strategic planning allows us to employ information rationally and to effectively make choices. Once those choices are made, we can turn our attention to our organization's operation. Who does what, by when, using what resources to move us from here to there? How do we build the right match between the various components of the organization? What has to happen inside to move us to the future we are looking for outside?

Phase 1: Data Collection

This is the first phase of strategic, long-range planning. In a knowledge-based enterprise data must be collected relevant to four information pools: (1) member needs, (2) industry foresight, (3) organizational position, and (4) ethical regulations. Information should provide a solid foundation for these areas to be discussed on an ongoing basis. Some information will come from data pools that are routinely created and maintained. Other information may need to be collected on an ad hoc basis, specifically relevant to the issue(s) being deliberated.

Phase 2: Direction Setting

This is the second phase of the process. An effective, strategic process can be modified based on new information, experiences, or changes in the environment on which the organization is focusing. We look at external trends, marketplace needs and preferences, and internal capabilities and resources. With this collection of information, we set direction. With constant, focused monitoring and adjustment we develop our action plan. Now we can constantly monitor the process and outcomes and adjust as we need to.

Importance of the Mission Statement

A strong mission statement clarifies the organization's service niche. Again, there are several elements to a good service niche: (1) it flows from a compelling vision; (2) this is supported by a mission and programs focused on high-priority needs of members; and (3) these member needs are of a type that the organization is positioned to respond to with excellence.

The mission statement should be a concise, precise, and, if possible, eloquent expression of the fundamental purpose for which the business exists. It states what is supposed to happen and for whom as a result of what the organization does. It is not merely a list of the business lines in which the organization is involved.

The mission statement is critical: everything involved in direction setting should be congruent with what it calls for. If an opportunity emerges that does not fit within the parameters of the mission statement, the organization should ask itself whether it is really an appropriate opportunity.

Strategies Aren't Always Purposeful

Organizations can sometimes execute strategy by accident. Every association has a strategy. It is the sum total of what it is doing. That does not mean that it is appropriate, conscious, or well-conceived.

Performance

Organizations produce output, represented by performance. Good strategic plans account for achieving performance through goals and objectives at three levels:

1. First, a good strategic plan considers performance of the organization at the association level.
2. Second, it considers performance of individual units or groups within the association. In a good strategic plan, roles and objectives can be constructed for each significant group or unit of work within the organization. Each is relevant to the big picture constructed for the association's members/customers. It is from here that strategic thrust is driven: the organization's vision of how the world will be different in a better way.
3. Third, an organization should not develop a plan based solely on its own picture of where it thinks it wants to go. Likewise, individuals in the organization should not develop their own performance objectives and job descriptions based only on their

own views of what they think they should be doing next. Those judgments should be made in the context of the organization's strategic plan. Knowledge-based systems allow opportunities for individuals to monitor the success of their own performance.

Participation Yields Progress

The process of strategic, long-range planning is as important as the product. To be effective, it must involve full participation of all parties as partners, senior staff and board, to produce easily understandable reports and documents. It must be linked to annual planning, budgeting, and evaluation. Meeting those criteria should result in formative, strategic, long-range planning. It should position an association to control its destiny, yield measurable progress to the delight of membership, and provide considerable satisfaction to the staff and member work force.

CHAPTER 11

Aligning Organizational Structures and Decision Processes

What has led to developing a new model of association organization in a knowledge-based environment? Driving this development has been a dramatic change in the nature of change itself. Associations need to manage change differently.

This dynamic affects two basic elements of the association environment: the structure of the organization and its decision processes. Because these have been based on a political model of governance used for over two hundred years, this historic model cannot move with sufficient speed to keep pace with the rapid and dramatic changes occurring in the arenas associations serve. This has led to a search for new ways to make association decision processes more knowledge based and less political.

Association Structures and Processes

There are four essential processes present, either formally or informally, in every association. They are (1) needs assessment, (2) strategic planning, (3) policy, and (4) budgeting. These processes are used to get significant work done.

Every association, society, or philanthropic or charitable enterprise is built on six elements of structure. They are:

1. Membership—The membership structure covers who can be a member, how members are organized, and what prerogatives they enjoy as a result of membership.
2. Governance—The governance structure is concerned with which units of thinking and decision making enjoy what authority and how people get to those units.
3. Program—The program structure includes major business lines, programs within those business lines, and specific activities and events within those programs.
4. Work force—The work force structure represents the ways the paid and voluntary work force are organized and how opportunities for interaction between the two are structured.

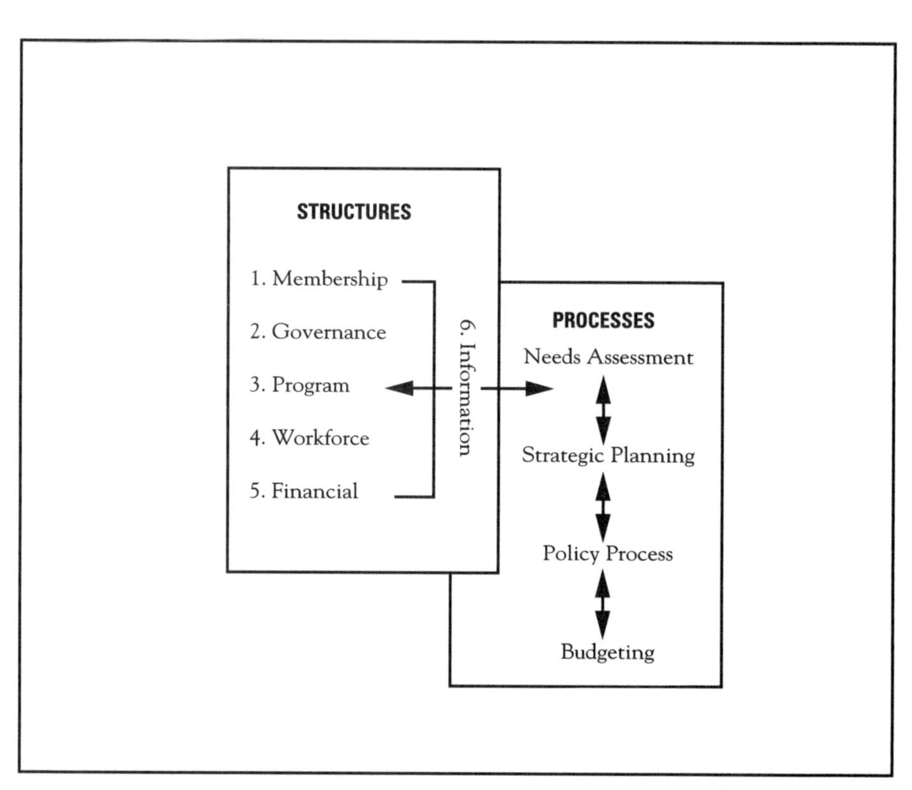

Figure 4. A Model of Association Infrastructure

5. Financial—Financial structure is not the budget. It is where resources come from and to what ends they are allocated.
6. Information—The information infrastructure is concerned with how people who are getting work done in each of the previous five elements access the insight, knowledge, and information they need to make good decisions or do good work. This represents the link between the other five elements of structure and the four processes. The information is generated in the processes and gets distributed to these elements of structure.

These are present in every not-for-profit, volunteer-intensive, often tax-exempt, service-oriented organization. Every association has all the parts. The issue is not whether you have a part, but whether you have the part working in a way that is well aligned with what you are trying to achieve.

How are Association Structures Changing?

Changes, evolutions, and new strategic directions occur in associations in each of these areas. It is useful here to revisit the three directions association structures are moving toward to adapt to increased volatility and unpredictability in their environments. They have needed to become: (1) more fluid, (2) more flexible, and (3) more responsive. It is a valuable exercise to examine these changes in your organization. What issues do they create, and how are you dealing with them?

More Fluid

The very structures of organizations have become amorphous. They have needed to adapt to changes in the dynamics of industries and in the professions' structures almost as rapidly as these have occurred. It is no longer practical for an organization to take a year or two to move through the committee process, to the executive committee, to the board, and then on to the house of delegates to get approval to allow, for example, an emerging new set of industry players, who do not fit into the existing membership eligibility requirements, to become part of the organization.

More Flexible

This has been required because needs and opportunities confronting members have been evolving faster than ever before. The organization has needed a way to quickly redistribute and reallocate assets and energies as new opportunities and challenges emerge. This has become more difficult as needs and expectations of each of the increasingly differing segments of the membership have, themselves, been changing very rapidly.

In the old model, by the time the organization got itself oriented to an emerging issue and got its assets actually converted into some constructive activity, that problem or opportunity usually had been replaced by a new one. The organization found itself, in the course of time, being perceived as a group that, at best, was always behind the curve.

More Responsive

The association has needed to become more responsive both to the needs of evolving membership and to the needs of the marketplace its members serve. It has had to move from being inner-directed (looking at only what members thought they wanted and needed) to being more outer-directed (anticipating what members' customers and

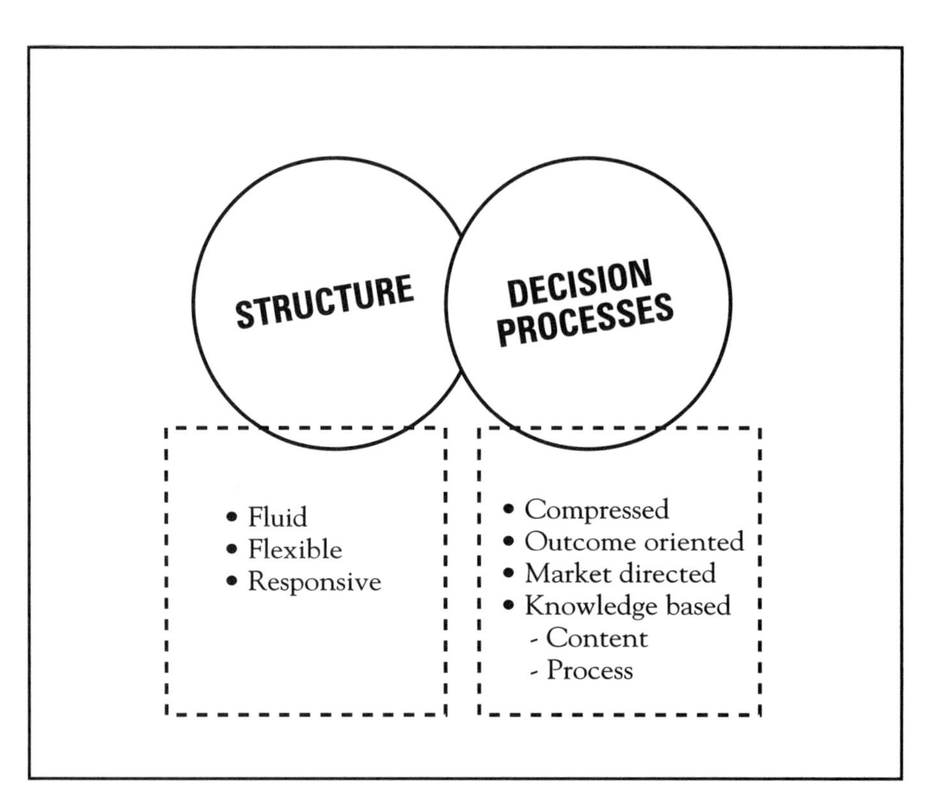

Figure 5. Implications of Change in the Nature of Change

marketplace would require). By doing this, for the first time, associations can make decisions about what they should be doing to position members to be more successful.

Knowledge-based organizations' decision processes have changed in three fundamental ways so structural changes can improve effectiveness.

1. *More compressed decision processes*. The time that elapsed between a need or opportunity being identified and something of real value actually happening for a member is dramatically shortened. Wait time has been eliminated.

2. *More outcome-oriented decision making*. Decisions made in the organization are premised on clarity and on the nature of the success being created for the member. Note: success is not being sought for the organization, but for the member.

3. *More market-directed*. This term now has a different meaning than it has had for the past five years in the association community. Market-directed no longer means

staff constantly polls and surveys the membership and then does whatever members perceive their interests, wants, and needs to be. Market directed now means leadership reaches through its membership into memberships' market, constantly collecting information allowing it to assess that market's current realities and evolving dynamics.

In sum, the organization's decision processes have become more knowledge based in two ways. First, it has built a methodology promoting decision making supported by expertise related to the decision's content. If an organization is making a decision about long-term investment, for example, then somebody who knows something about long-term investments is included in the decision group.

Second, the very process of decision making has become more knowledge based. Now, not only does the organization seek content knowledge about investments, but it also seeks expertise about the steps required to make good decisions about long-term investment strategy. The knowledge-based association has present decision-making expertise related to both the subject of the decision and the process of making that decision.

Moving the organization in these two areas begins to create a new character and ultimately change the culture of the organization. Some constructs examined here may look a bit like other things you have heard of, like coalitions or federations, but the change in the way work takes place dramatically alters the organization's culture. It moves it away from the government-based model of decision making to a more businesslike process. This is an essential ingredient of a new model for organizations serving any shifting industry.

Marketing and Market-Directed Processes

In a knowledge-based approach, a strong marketing effort requires knowing:

- written communications alone do not equal effective communication (communicating activities and features is not marketing);
- internal marketing is not a traditional membership development activity, and external marketing does not mean only advertising;
- how to market in terms of benefits and value-added benefits, not features and activities (for example, does your association's new member brochure describe activities or benefits?);

- how to reshape staff and volunteer committees to consolidate all association marketing functions and activities into a core resource structure that features: (1) well-planned marketing outcomes; (2) a coordinated marketing thrust; (3) a single, recognizable message; and (4) carefully identified, target audiences;
- internal marketing also includes annual reports, membership assessment, and so on;
- external marketing includes new member attraction, community relations, media and industry relations, and targeted public relations;
- most associations do not have resources to increase their image to society at large;
- how to contract for outside assistance if the association internally lacks the marketing skills and expertise; and
- how to grow the right mix of internal skills and expertise.

Needs Assessment Capabilities and Processes

A knowledge-based enterprise understands the need to be sensitive to members' view of the world and then to blend that sensitivity with other important insights. It is important to understand the limitations of membership assessment. Members can tell you exactly what they want, but they often do not have a clear idea about what they need.

In a knowledge-based approach, successful assessment is accomplished by asking members to look out and forward at their industry or their profession. They should look out into the future and tell you what they see, not just give their opinion of present conditions or degree of satisfaction with existing programs. For example, are there three or four strategic issues they think will impact the future?

There is an almost endless number of techniques associations can use for qualitative and quantitative assessment including written surveys, focus groups, town meetings, and fax surveys. The key here is to select the appropriate one.

Different types of membership assessments have advantages or disadvantages depending on what you want to know and who you want to talk to get the information. Knowledge-based decision making requires the right match between

1. what decision you want to be able to make;
2. what information you will need;
3. the source(s) of that information;
4. the best way to collect the information from that source(s);

5. the way the information will be tabulated and analyzed; and
6. to whom it will be reported and interpreted.

Driving this process is the fact that associations no longer have single homogeneous memberships with the same wants and needs. Memberships are really made up of a number of constituencies or segments. If membership is analyzed, it can be broken into subgroups by geography, age brackets, type of profession, specialty, size of business, etc.

Creating Flexible Organizational Structures

Like many organizations in the for-profit sector, associations, over time, have grown around the need for functional structures. As new program and service areas were added, functional departments were built to support their requirements. As a result, most associations have evolved into organizational structures with very separate areas focusing on member services, education, information systems, finance, government relations, and other areas.

The drawback of structures of this sort, as has been discovered in the private sector, is that an organizational culture of "silos" has developed. Each area or department has organized and prioritized around its area of responsibility, and the ability to address issues that cut across functional boundaries has been limited.

In a knowledge-based association, the structure of the organization becomes less focused on departments with functional responsibilities and more on work processes and outcomes. Functional areas of responsibility may remain, but shared accountabilities are established across organizational boundaries. For example, the process of membership needs assessment, in the past, has often fallen into marketing or membership services. But in reality, every functional area of an association is gathering valuable information about members needs, wants, and expectations. In a knowledge-based organization, this information is shared across the organization.

Engaging in an honest, self-appraisal of the current condition of your association may make you intellectually uncomfortable. Nonetheless, consider it a learning opportunity. Keep in mind that commitment to necessary change often grows from discomfort. Poor or faulty alignment in an organization indicates some change is needed.

Aligning Working Parts

Alignment is the fit between the parts of the organization that are actually doing work. There are some peculiarities about associations as enterprises that have specific implications related to alignment.

One of the distinct differences between associations and for-profit enterprises is that, in an association, most of the work force is not employed by the organization. Executors of work processes are not employees but, in many cases, bosses. This peculiarity makes how we go about doing things significantly different from other places where members may have had experiences.

Another distinguishing feature of associations is that they must focus on membership's common self interests. This relates to alignment, how the working parts fit together, as well as installing an approach to quality in those working parts.

As noted earlier, an association's members are becoming less like each other instead of becoming more like each other. This increase in segmentation of membership, resulting in populations of members with different expectations, needs, experiences, preferences, and attitudes, has significant implications for the way work gets done. As members become more and more different from each other, associations need to construct a larger variety of ways for work to get done. This needs to be accomplished in a way that still makes all working parts of the organization fit together and work in a common direction toward an agreed upon outcome. This understanding becomes even more apparent when looking at the dynamics affecting an association's membership as a whole (see figure 2).

A Detailed Look

How effectively is your association aligned? Knowledge of organizational dynamics is essential to make decisions about alignment because this does not occur in a vacuum. Associations operate in a variety of arenas in which there is constant change and shifting. There are internal changes in membership, while simultaneously there are continuous changes in the environment in which members function. When there is a change in the demographics of the membership's marketplace, in an association's work force, or in your membership, then there is a significant change in members' needs.

When legislation or regulation creates a significant change in your members' environment, then there is also a significant change in members' needs. Change in how work gets done, either by you or by your members, driven by technology or science, creates significant changes in members' needs. Change in natural resources, human resources, and in values of attendant and relative communities, also create significant changes in your members' needs.

Managing Through Change

Change in the dynamics of the organization that you lead is not a solitary event or phenomenon but is continuous. Your primary role over the next decade and into the twenty-first century could be characterized as helping your association manage through change. It is not possible to manage change—there are simply too many variables over which we have little control. It is possible, however, for us to manage through change. This can be done most successfully by aligning the working parts of your organization in a way that lets you establish conditions, increase fluidity, and become beneficially opportunistic.

Associations successful in the twenty-first century will have fluid organizational alignment. These organizations will be strategic tools, in themselves, for getting work accomplished that needs to be done to achieve desired outcomes.

Second, they will become increasingly opportunistic. Organizational structures must preserve appropriate distributions of authority and responsibility, but be able to respond almost instantaneously to opportunities to provide quality service or support to members. Being fluid and opportunistic suggests certain alignments creating the opportunity for responsive flexibility.

Responsive Flexibility

When members' needs have been determined, direction can be set. Direction is articulated in an organization's mission, goals, and strategies. Once direction is set, decisions can be made on the kind of work needed. That work is reflected in programs and services. When a determination has been made about what work needs to get done, then decisions are made about how it can get done most efficiently—about organizing and what operating and support systems will be required.

It is foolish to make decisions about how work will get done without first having decided what kind of work needs to get done. It is illogical to make important decisions about how resources will be allocated to do work if you have not first decided what that work is.

These are issues of efficiency and effectiveness. There is a critical difference between the two. Understanding this difference gives you critical insight for making good decisions about alignment and its effective use to execute quality programs. If you are concerned about efficiency, the question you are asking and answering is, "Am I doing things right?" If you are concerned about effectiveness, the question you are asking and answering is, "Am I doing the right thing?"

The Organizational Alignment Model

Critical processes are, again, the strategic planning process, policy process, and the needs assessment or market research process (that creates the common information base used in making decisions for the other vehicles), and the budgeting process. Merely, re-engineering processes without considering the behaviors (culture) needed to execute them well is not likely to lead to a knowledge-based system.

When any of these inter-related elements are poorly aligned, the entire organization can be out of alignment. To draw a metaphor, picture a car where one part of the car involved in steering faces a different direction than another part involved in steering. If the right tire, your executive committee, is facing a different direction, you are going to end up somewhere other than where you want to be. If the back of the chassis, your policy committee, is facing another direction, again, you probably will end up somewhere other than where you want to be. Coordinated thrust becomes impossible where there is a deficiency or mismatch in any of these structures and processes.

Consider this on two levels. One is the extent to which you currently have a match, given the work you are doing today. The second is the extent to which you have an appropriate match, given the work you anticipate you will be doing tomorrow. In the first instance you need to think about whether decisions are being made efficiently and work is getting carried out to accomplish today's goals. In the second instance, you also need to think about whether you have such efficiencies in your process to successfully do your work tomorrow. Fluidity and the ability to be opportunistic are necessary ingredients.

Organizational alignment requires special attention to three things. First, the behavior of people; second, the fit of the structures and processes of the organization; and third, the extent to which there is a match between allocating resources through these processes and the commitments made to the kind of work that needs to get done.

In a knowledge-based approach, alignment is addressed in strategic planning. Few things can better remedy the vulnerabilities of your organization than effectively constructed strategic planning. If your strategic planning process does not give adequate consideration to alignment issues, then you may want, as a first leadership initiative, to alter or enhance the planning process itself.

How, specifically, can the issue of alignment manifest itself in an association? The organizational productivity model (figure 6) does not portray either a healthy or an unhealthy organization. It is a picture of the elements of any organization that, together, can make it either healthy or unhealthy in varying degrees. This picture lets you focus on specific details of the four components that constitute what you are doing with the "stuff that comes in."

It is in the relationship of these four components and the efficiency that occurs in each of them that alignment, either bad or good, takes place. (See Tecker and Fidler 1993 for additional information and practical tools for conducting such analysis.) The extent to which this portrait is satisfactory or comfortable for you demonstrates the extent to which your association exhibits the conditions needed for effective execution of a quality management, total employee involvement, or quality assurance program.

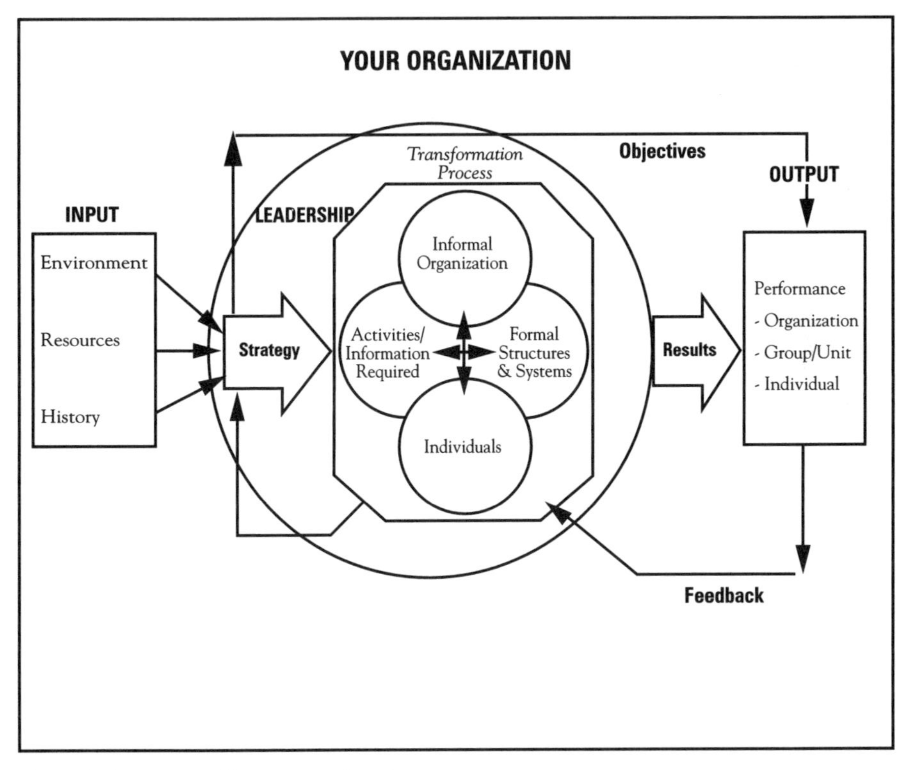

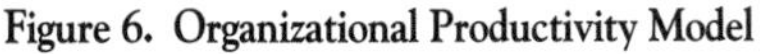
Figure 6. Organizational Productivity Model

Leadership involves behaviors essential for guiding the actual work of individuals so they can carry out activities in ways compatible with strategy. The strategy itself includes integrating resources, capacities, and competencies of the organization in a way that creates a coordinated thrust toward described outcomes.

Four Components of Strategy

Strategy describes how an organization takes advantage of its capacities and how it will work with each of four special components. These components move the organization where leadership said it wanted the organization to go, in a way that differentiates it from other organizations.

Component One: Work

This first core component area includes the knowledge and skills the organization and individuals require to effectively do what they have been assigned. It also concerns information they require to do it well and how that information is analyzed, interpreted, and processed for them. It includes the extent to which information is turned into usable knowledge for them by the organization.

It also has to do with inherent rewards, the extent to which what they like to do and do well is well matched to what they are being asked to do. Leaders must focus on members, staff, and their integrated output. A harsh reality association executives face after just a few months on the job is that, no matter whether the organization depends on a member or a paid employee to get the work done, if the work does not get done, the effect on the organization is the same.

Component Two: Formal Structures and Systems

The second of the four primary components is represented by formal structures and systems. This includes grouping—how things are organized for decisions to be made. This links relationships among the working parts of the organization and the physical environment. It refers to the quality and appropriateness of the space that has been provided within which the work must get done.

Along with structures, systems are assessed. Systems for work include the methods and practices that you expect, policies, rules, and procedures and guidelines. They also include information technology and the extent to which access has been created to the knowledge required to get work done. It includes support systems represented by the extent to which temporary tools have been provided to workers so they can effectively get work done.

In addition to these systems for work there are the systems for people. The systems for people include unit resource management systems—how judgments are made related to the match of people and work, peoples' performance, and the outcomes required and the quality of behavior exhibited while work is performed. Reward systems are included here—what really encourages that baggage handler? Is it a compensation program where base salary is premised on time and longevity or is there a group incentive bonus premised on units of baggage handled per hour? Review this component and decide whether it is an area of strength, competence, or need in your own organization. Discover places where there is good or poor alignment.

Component Three: Informal Organization

The third of the four components is the informal organization, or the *real* policy manual of the place. The informal organization has to do with interpersonal relationships, cliques, coalitions, informal working arrangements, norms, and values. This is the third of the three circles of mission, operations, and group process.

Component Four: Individuals

The last of the four components is the component of individuals, also known as where "the rubber meets the road." This refers to both staff and elected leadership. The organization's dependency on someone to get the work done draws no distinction between volunteers or paid staff members. This component involves assessing knowledge and skills—not the possession of knowledge and skills, but the ways they are exhibited in executing work to meet needs, values, and to reward fulfilled expectations.

Because all of these elements are interrelated, it would be inappropriate to say any one of them is any more or less important. However, given the culture, context, and issues confronting organizations, these elements take on varying importance at different times.

You can establish a rough estimate of the relative health of your organization by summing its strengths, competencies, and needs. Your overall strategy as a leader should be to preserve the strengths, build up the competencies so they do not degenerate into weaknesses, and remedy any existing weaknesses.

To achieve good, productive alignment, every level of work is important. If incompetence in the mailroom creates a situation where a carefully crafted communication does not get to the person with whom you are trying to communicate, the significance and effect of that misfit is raised, perhaps even above the level of the executive's contribution.

Evolving Elements of Association Infrastructure

Maintaining alignment is an issue of continuing concern in a dynamic environment. Knowledge-based organizations will routinely reassess the match between current assumptions about the key structures pictured in table 6 and shifts in their relevant environments. Changes in organizational structure and process are likely to be necessitated by significant changes in memberships' world. Such changes are occurring more frequently in many environments, and it is likely this pattern will continue.

Knowledge-based organizations will need to be capable of executing the political and operational changes necessary to remain responsive in an increasingly fluid context.

While many major trends affecting an association are specific to the industry, profession, or common interest arena of the organization, some changes are generically relevant to all not-for-profits. Trends affecting the unique nature of not-for-profit enterprises are already observable.

Membership Structure

One of the things now discernible across most not-for-profit organizations is substantially less concern about who can be a member. This is particularly true in organizations serving professions, industries, or issue areas where it is becoming difficult to predict who is going to be involved in the organization.

Fewer Rules

Some associations are serving industries/professions that are restructuring. New groups are becoming key players in traditional industry activities. When it is difficult to predict who potential members will be, organizations pay less attention to developing rules in this area.

This is where an extraordinary paradigm shift is occurring. Associations have always determined what they should be doing by asking three specific questions in a particular order. Who are our members, what are their needs, and, therefore, what should we be doing?

When an organization moves away from creating a large number of rules dictating membership, the paradigm shifts to a new set of questions in a different order. First, what goals and outcomes are we trying to achieve? Second, what kind of work will we need to do to achieve them? Third, who might be interested in being part of this?

Traditional Structures More Ambiguous

A second paradigm shift is that traditional structures within the membership structure are becoming less important. This is movement to an ambiguity that allows such associations to create a variety of ways in which people can be involved.

The office products industry provides a prime example of this. Among other things, the office products industry re-identified itself as the "business products industry." The reason for that was that a great deal of business does not take place in an office anymore, but in the home. That was change one.

A second change was in industry membership. Remember that, for many years, the office products industry membership structure consisted of "mom and pop" retail stores, and the association governance structure was aligned that way. Mom and pop office products retailers got together in every state and selected some leaders. Those leaders got together regionally, and some of them would be selected to be regional representatives to the national organization.

Program structure served the needs of mom and pop stores. There were a couple of publications and videotapes that talked about the latest merchandise and how to manage staff. Special services included insurance programs for liability and property and casualty coverage.

The association work force structure was composed of a series of standing committees consisting of mom and pop owners from across the country. There were standing committees for education, publications, insurance, and others.

Again, as mentioned earlier, unexpectedly and very quickly, along came Staples, Office Depot, and OfficeMax, capturing a huge percent of the market previously serviced by the mom and pop members of the industry. This caused a problem for the industry's association because it did not have a good way for these new players to be members.

They had to reinvent their membership structure. They created a variety of comfortable homes for different groups that might be interested in becoming involved in the association's initiatives. There was a home for the multi-state, large firm, which was very different in how it worked and what it did from the home defined for the surviving mom and pop enterprises.

Table 6. Synopsis of Infrastructure Elements and Trends

Element	Key Components	Implications of Trends
Concept	• A broad description of the proposed model	
Membership Structure	• Who can be or choose to be a member, how membership groups are classified and organized, and the rights and prerogatives enjoyed by various membership categories • May also include degree of centralness—understanding who are the organization's core members, members, customers, and key stakeholders	*Associations will become less concerned with who can be a member and more concerned with what populations will be attracted to involvement in their programs and policy initiatives.*
Program Structure	• Business lines, programs, specific events or activities—the work of the association	*Increased segmentation of membership populations and increasing diversity in member preferences will require a high degree of competence in planning and program delivery.*
Governance Structure	• Decision-making units of the organization and the relative powers, authorities, and responsibilities each possesses • The composition of each unit and how individuals are selected to participate in them	*Many governance systems will need to be streamlined in a world that requires more decisions be made more quickly and with better knowledge*
Work Force Structure	• The human resource pool—both volunteer and employed • Committee system, staff divisions or departments, relationships with outside experts and contractors	*The rate of change will require tomorrow's associations to be highly responsive, flexible, and fluid in work force structure—to be able to quickly re-focus assets on a rapidly evolving and frequently shifting set of priorities. Communication abilities needed to ensure constancy of direction and coherency of program in such a rapidly changing organizational environment will be a challenge.*
Financial and Dues Structure	• Sources of revenue, relative proportions of revenue from various sources, the allocation and placement of available revenue, and the anticipated cost of resources and opportunities over time • Includes dues structures, investment strategies, and projected estimates of significant costs • Basic decisions related to fiscal status and selection of tax-exempt status (e.g., 501 c3 vs. 501 c6) are determinations about financial structure with enormous strategic implications	*Association leaders will increasingly need sophisticated skills in acquiring and using specialized information to effectively consider strategic implications of financial structures in a rapidly paced marketplace. Interpersonal skills, especially those related to managing group processes, will be essential to facilitating groups working with a sometimes unpredictably shifting spectrum of resource allocation decisions with complex technical and political implications.*

Table 6. Synopsis of Infrastructure Elements and Trends *(Continued)*

Element	Key Components	Implications of Trends
Information and Knowledge Structure	• Links the structures of the association to its decision-making processes. • Ensures that individuals and groups executing activity have the information and knowledge they require to make sound decisions and effectively execute work. Includes (1) the decisions that will be needed at each and all levels of the organization; (2) the data and information that will be required to effectively make those decisions; (3) the sources of that data and information; (4) the systems for collecting the information from appropriate sources; (5) the methods for tabulation and analysis that aggregate and categorize the information; (6) the hardware, software, systems, and processes that will be used to interpret the information, integrate it with the appropriate know how, and systematically distribute or provide access to it in useful forms to the person or places that will need to make or coordinate judgments based on it.	*A new set of competencies related to interaction with information will be required of leaders to function effectively in the future. Much of the future nature, organization, manipulation, and application of information that will be potentially relevant to association leaders is still unknown. The ability to learn to use various information in a variety of forms and ways that may not yet be conceived will be necessary.*
Core Competencies	• The consolidation of technologies and skills into competencies that empower the organization to adapt quickly to changing opportunities • Core competencies should: (1) provide potential access to a wide variety of markets (segments and services), and (2) be difficult for competitors to imitate	*Based on core competencies, an organization can identify its service niche, that is, those services that the organization is uniquely positioned to provide.*
Needs Assessment Process	• A variety of data collection methodologies employed in a coherent strategy to continuously collect and interpret information about membership, programs, and the larger world within which members are functioning • May include such activities as written, electronic, or telephone survey; personal or telephone interviews; focus group research; assessment of member behavior by analysis of an accurate behavioral data base; and a variety of other market research-like technologies	

Table 6. Synopsis of Infrastructure Elements and Trends *(Continued)*

Element	Key Components	Implications of Trends
Strategic Planning Process	• A continuous process of thoughtfully determining direction, at all levels of the organization, on the basis of careful assessment of clearly defined and desired outcomes • Usually includes basic phases of (1) data collection; (2) direction setting; (3) strategy development for programs, organization structure and process, finance and technology; (4) action planning to guide implementation and accountability; and (5) monitoring and adjusting as events in the larger world, new information, or experience in implementing strategy suggest the need for change	
Policy Setting Process	• Involves established and clear procedures for rational deliberation • Defines the intellectual and political steps participants take to produce judgments related to (1) positions the organization takes on public issues of importance to the membership or (2) statements of direction, guidelines, or parameters established as frameworks within which operations are to be executed. Includes systematic procedures for maintaining written, easily accessible documentation of policy determinations made by all units of the organization with policy-level authority.	
Financial Planning/ Budgeting Process	• Systematic analysis of needs, opportunities, capacity, and strategic position—linked to a strategic plan	*These four basic decision-making processes (needs, opportunities, capacity, and strategic position) will undergo dramatic changes in the future. These processes will be at the heart of success or failure for many organizations as they seek to manage through change.*

There is an opposite side to this. There are associations, particularly professional societies, that have gone through periods of time where they worked hard to establish professional status for their members and where one of the strategies used was to make membership exclusive or elite. A candidate had to hold a certain kind of credential, do a certain amount of work, and had spent a certain amount of time involved in being a certain kind of person. That was a good strategy for establishing professional identity, and it was successful.

The problem it created, however, is that product, service, and leadership must be continuously provided to those groups. A great deal of work goes into maintaining stringent eligibility requirements. This might be comparable to being a Nordstrom's shopper: there are a great number of rules shoppers have to be willing to follow before they can shop there. You can bet that most of those customers will look for a place with easier access.

Organizations tend to do something similar with membership. They create rules for participation. The question becomes whether the existence of those rules is still of strategic value, even to a traditional membership that can often benefit by having access to the perceptions of those outside the traditional member population. They certainly would benefit if those outsiders could be converted into partners who could join in pursuing issues the organization is advocating.

Hybrid or More Flexible Structures

This leads to another trend, increased flexibility in membership structures and hybrid structures. Philanthropic organizations may be years ahead of trade and professional associations in this regard because they have always managed leadership and membership structures. The only common interest held by people in philanthropic organizations has been a commitment to the particular arena in which they were operating. They had to look for individuals willing to give a lot of work and, also, for other individuals willing to give support in terms of assets.

Involving Prospective Members

Another trend is recognition of populations that will be attracted to involvement in programs and policy initiatives. Here, the notion of core members (figure 7) and members and customers becomes important. Opportunities are created for people to become actively involved in the association's work even if they are not members. It is a value to the organization to have access to them, their energy, time, dollars, and expertise.

As often as not, you can find working committees, usually ad hoc in nature, composed of many individuals or experts who are not organization members at all. This is also a paradigm shift in the culture of many associations. It is a big change from the habit of thinking in terms of insiders or outsiders or members or non-members. "Non-member" is no longer a good expression to use. Much better and more appropriate is the term "prospective member" unless you want to disregard important potential.

Changes in membership structure are linked to changes in governance structure. Organizations customarily tried to make sure governance reflected the different segments of population present in the membership. The belief was that if each of those segments had a place in governance, fairness would exist.

There are definite effects on governance structure when the traditional paradigm for membership structures is abandoned. Where will leaders come from? In a knowledge-based culture, they may not come from traditional political populations. They are likely to come from places where intellectual capital exists.

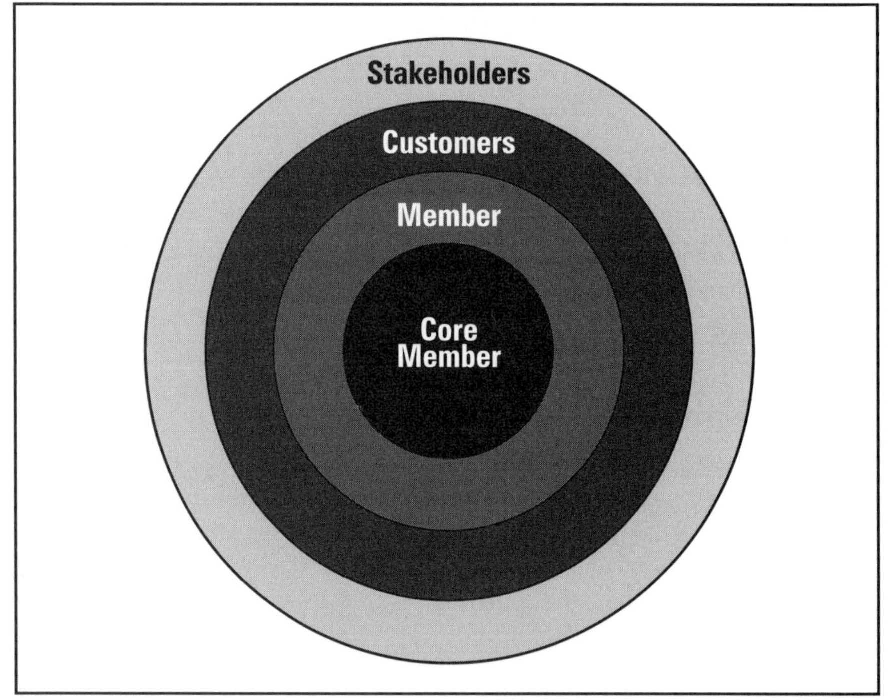

Figure 7. Core Members

Governance Structure Changes

Another trend is streamlining the governance structure for decisions to be made more quickly and with better knowledge. When technologies, like critical path analysis, are used to look at how decisions are actually getting made, they often reveal a common dynamic.

Wait Time

A certain amount of time always elapses between the point when somebody has a really good idea, to when the idea gets translated into something tangible—when, finally, a member actually gets some benefit. As mentioned earlier, in most associations, the proportion of the time actually consumed by someone doing real work between the time a good idea is generated and somebody benefits from it, is about 20 percent.

Again, that 80 percent or more of time between those two points that does not involve real work is "wait time." You are waiting for somebody else to say "Yes." You are waiting for somebody else, who really does not even have authority to say "Yes" or "No," to give an opinion. You are waiting for data from somebody else that you depend on because you do not have it yourself. Most often, you are waiting for a base to be touched with some group you believe is politically related to making the decision, but which is not really related to the content of the decision.

When wait time is examined, you almost always find that it is produced by a series of controls that are in place but which bring no additional value to the decision. If decision-making processes are needed that are more nimble, fluid, flexible, quick, and streamlined, and you want to streamline without sacrificing participation or the appropriate authority invested in a group, you will have to figure out how to reduce wait time.

If the wait time is, in large measure, due to a series of controls that add no value to the decision, get rid of them. These cannot just be abandoned, though, they must be replaced with something more beneficial.

These controls must be replaced with trust. If this can be done, then wait time can be off-loaded and the governance process streamlined without sacrificing either participation or authority. For trust to occur, two things are needed, at a minimum. You need clarity and consensus on what constitutes success, and you need to articulate the outcomes you are trying to achieve. If you articulate the outcomes you are trying to achieve, then oversight is exercised by seeing if things are working, not by watching how they are getting done.

Clarity on Success

When you have taken the time to reach clarity and consensus on what will constitute success, the outcomes, issue by issue, assignment by assignment, are clear. In this case, you do not just give a committee a charge; you make sure the committee also has a series of tangible objectives to achieve—specific products you expect by a certain point in time. These could be a recommendation, a study, a new program, it does not matter. It is not just a charge; however, it is a set of objectives you have negotiated together.

Both parties know what they are trying to accomplish by achieving those objectives. Now you are able to provide oversight, leaving the committee to its work and, together, finding places where both you and the committee can stop to assess progress toward the outcomes both parties seek. Assessment is not done to document a problem, but to see whether progression is satisfactory. If it is not, you are able to alter what you are doing to increase the probability of success.

This difference between oversight and supervision, together with the need to be clear on outcomes you are after, can be applied organizationally. They are the ingredients critical to achieving a knowledge-based environment characterized by trust and the elimination of unnecessary controls.

Open Access to Information

Trust only occurs in organizations where there is reasonably open access to deliberations about what you are doing, why you are doing it, and how well you are doing. In a knowledge-based organization, this is enabled by systems for exchanging information and insights and by use of "informed intuition" and "dialogue before deliberation" in decision making.

It is essential to earn a climate of trust in a knowledge-based operational philosophy. This enables elimination of wait time due to useless controls, thereby streamlining the decision-making process, and, also, making possible down sizing of decision groups.

Many associations are moving to making every level of decision-making smaller, not larger, and they are able to do it without sacrificing participation. By using a variety of technologies, they allow broader groups of members to engage in deliberations that create information bases on which decisions are made. Every time the smaller board of directors says, "Here's what we've decided and here's why," they are also able to say, "and we decided it on the basis of what you said you wanted us to do," thereby streamlining while preserving participation.

A discernible trend, related to this, is pushing down authority to get it closer to where activity is occurring. For trade associations, this is more comfortable because most for-profit industries are moving in this direction. For professional societies, this is more difficult because they are made up of entrepreneurial individuals who have their hands in everything.

The effort, here, is to get higher levels of authority that reside in more important roles down to smaller groups that are able to meet more frequently and, therefore, assimilate more information to make decisions about more targeted sets of things. That is a shortcut, but the direction is clear.

Membership expects the organization to use credible information when making decisions. Considering the four knowledge-based questions (sensitivity to members; foresight into the likely evolution of their environment; insight into the organization's capacity and strategic position; and consideration of the ethical dimensions of choices) demonstrates movement toward knowledge-based decision making, both formal and informal.

Synergy and Consensus

There is increasing movement to decision making through synergy and consensus rather than compromise. This may sound pretty esoteric. As mentioned earlier, most associations have historically used a political model for governance. Now, though, they are sliding closer to a more rational or information-based model of decision making.

Effective governance and progress come through synergy and consensus, not compromise. In a political model, several people get together and put a lot of stuff on the table for consideration. One by one, they take stuff off the table until they get to the point where at least one more than 50 percent of those voting can agree to what is left on the table because they do not strongly object to it.

That is a compromise. As mentioned earlier, the problem is that, frequently, compromise is really the lowest common denominator. What is left on the table, while not offensive to 51 percent of the voters, may not be related at all to what the group really should be doing.

In the synergistic model, rather than approach with the pejorative sense of compromise, you begin discussions by announcing what you are trying to achieve and by getting clarity and consensus on those outcomes. That lets the discussion revolve around who needs to do what and who can contribute what to make satisfactory progress toward the outcomes that represent the common good. With outcome orientation in governance comes the ability to move further from a political model to a more knowledge-based model.

Consider the balance. Where you are engaged in advocacy, the political model is probably appropriate. But where you are engaged in decision making about programs and services, the political model may not be the right way to make the decisions. The synergistic, more businesslike, knowledge-based model would be the best choice.

Program Structure Changes

Changes are occurring in program structure. There is increased segmentation of membership and more diversity among member preferences. Membership is getting even more disparate than what it is looking for, and there is increased member demand for value.

Because of these factors, many associations are using structures where programming is deliberately designed to meet the needs of certain targeted groups. Both content of programs and the delivery or access systems are being more and more customized for particular groups.

Doing fewer things of higher value to more targeted groups of people is likely to be the strategy of choice into the twenty-first century for many associations. By decreasing the breadth of what they offer, associations will be able to provide more ways to access the things they do best. This is especially important if they are developing alliances with other groups that provide responses to members' high priority needs. Your organization may not need to develop the internal capacity to be a direct provider. Offering fewer things of higher value for more targeted groups of people allows the association to decrease large initiatives with diffused relevance.

This does not mean that the day of your annual meeting or trade exhibit is over. These events will still be needed to create that special sense of community in the organization. What also is happening is that associations are building program matrices within their annual meetings where attendees can follow a track based either on the subject matter or the particular function or role they play in their industry or profession. Even where virtual systems are diminishing the need for people to gather together to learn or to work, considerable need will still exist.

Work Force Structure Changes

Along with program structure, significant changes are taking place in work force structures that are becoming more responsive, more flexible, and more fluid. This is allowing the organization to quickly re-focus its assets on rapidly evolving and changing priorities.

This represents an abandonment of the traditional bureaucracy of standing committees. It is a movement toward "adhocracies" (ad-hoc, problem-solving work groups outside the normal bureaucracy of the organization). It is also a movement toward uncoupling committee, staff, and program structure.

Undoubtedly, the future will require staff to do some things that members have done, simply because members have less time and less technical expertise required to do some things that are not within their primary fields. For example, if an association of worm farmers makes a commitment to develop some technological access to business information, it is not very likely that they will have the technical expertise to serve on a committee and make a good decision about what technology infrastructure is right.

The relationship between work force structure and program structure causes things to happen in the organization. An organization with a standing committee of members for every major program of the association, every business line, and/or every division for which there is staff will have conflicting parallel structures.

When a standing committee has responsibility for an area that a staff division is working on, chances are high that the committee will forget that its job is to provide recommendations and advice. As time passes, they may get a little confused and end up believing their job is to direct program and strategy in that area.

When this happens, a mini board of directors exists for each staff division. Certain staff members develop political constituencies within the membership—this tends to show up at budget time. In such circumstances, the parallel structures are driving the organization toward being member-directed, but not in a good way.

In a knowledge-based enterprise, these relationships would be uncoupled. "Adhocracies" would be developed, and members would come together to effectively focus on strategy and programs that achieve certain objectives. Staff silos would be eliminated, and staff teams with multiple expertise would be developed. Their expertise would be combined to work toward achieving objectives.

The relationship between the work force structure in staff and the work force structure in committees is important. To the extent that you wish to be political, parallel structures are created. To the extent that you would like to be more knowledge based, these two structures are uncoupled.

Predict Consequences

Exercise care when you consider implementing any of these changes. Each of these strategic directions and trends can get very different results when applied to different associations. Although their directions appear generic, they manifest themselves in a variety of forms. Try to predict the consequences before you make the moves.

CHAPTER 12

The Interrelationship of Culture and Competency

In a knowledge-based association, the senior staff and the top member leaders exercise oversight responsibility for creating and sustaining an enabling culture for the organization through a consultative partnership. Staff and member leaders are "keepers of the soul" of the organization. Today's members, especially younger members who want to become and remain involved, need to feel good about their association, what it does, and how it does it. The association's soul lies in its culture.

New competition for programs and services makes it strategically necessary for associations to position themselves as attractive, enjoyable communities. Programs and services are still important, but these needs are increasingly being met by non-association sources. A sense of being a "community of practice," "community of commitment," or "community of common self interest" is a distinguishing characteristic for an association.

Building and Sustaining an Enabling Culture

If your members were asked, "How do you feel about your association?" the answer would unambiguously reveal how they perceive your culture. If they answer,

- "It's a very progressive association, it meets my needs and wants, and I feel pretty good about belonging to it," or
- "It's really starting to get to be 'a day late and a dollar short'—I'm feeling less comfortable about belonging to it. In fact, I'm really not sure why I even wrote the check this year,"

you get a pretty clear-cut picture of the perceived status of the organization.

In a member or prospective member's mind, what makes sustaining culture increasingly complex, and, ironically, increasingly important, is that there exists greater diversity among members than ever before, and it is simultaneously becoming more difficult and more important to cement diverse populations together.

Core Ideology

Core ideology holds an association together. It consists of core purpose, as reflected in the organization's mission and core values. The organization's mission and core values describe the assumptions and beliefs of the organization, which represent the common understandings and commitments of those who have voluntarily chosen to associate together.

Common demography, needs, and goals are important. The essential source of commonality, however, is core values. Where core values are not sufficiently common, associations will separate, splinter, or face constant, paralyzing conflict. As membership diversifies, the need to create and sustain an enabling culture becomes more important.

If culture is the unwritten fabric of the organization, what are its threads? They are made up of the specific beliefs, assumptions, and values influencing how people behave in the organization.

Think about what happens when you go to a new job. During that first week or so, you are trying to do many things. Part of what you do is try to find out how you are supposed behave. You are not seeking information about what is written in the policies and the procedures manuals, but about what to do when you want something done. Who do you really talk to? How do you dress? What is appropriate to talk about when you have coffee? What is not? What outsiders are perceived as good guys, and who are the bad guys? All this represents the organization's culture. It is not written down, but members and prospective members know what it is when they encounter it.

Culture is very important to consider when undertaking change. If culture is not considered, fierce resistance will probably be generated, reflected in classic quotes like, "Yeah, but this is how we've always done things around here."

Beliefs and Assumptions, Values and Behavior

In associations that begin the journey to a knowledge-based operational philosophy, significant change in both organizational culture and competencies can be expected. The basic elements of culture that will be effected include:

- *Beliefs and assumptions:* the view of the world that people in the organization have
- *Values:* what they consider to be most important because of that view
- *Behavior:* the actions they actually execute based on their beliefs and assumptions and those values

The knowledge-based culture is the most comfortable environment for the consultative partnership, which needs to exist between staff and elected leadership for them to function effectively. That is why you need to take a hard look at the relationships between your organization's culture and competencies. Ask yourself, honestly: What is your association like? Do you really have the competencies required to operate an association exhibiting the characteristics of a knowledge-based enterprise? Do you really have a culture that enables the effective execution of those competencies?

Significant Change Area One: Communication and Information

Who has the obligation to make sure two-way communication is successful? The people you are talking to or the people doing the talking? The answer is both, but the greatest responsibility lies with the individual or group who has the need to be understood. The moment responsibility for clarity and sufficiency of communications is shifted to the person you are trying to talk to is the moment you lose the attention necessary to ensure your communications are clear enough to achieve your objectives.

In the twenty-first century, access to and distribution of information will generate power. Information interdependencies among groups will be created so common success, in large measure, will depend on benefiting from several sets of wisdom. The more people interdependent on the knowledge you offer, the more power you will possess in that environment.

There will be practical exceptions to this. If an organization is building a program, it will not want its competitor to know what it is planning. If you are developing a political strategy to execute a campaign, you certainly do not want the opposition to know what your arguments will be and, thereby, to give them time to prepare to counter them. While there will be exceptions, on the whole, this represents a huge paradigm shift. Knowledge-based associations will benefit from a culture that enhances and acts on this shift.

Significant Change Area Two: Leadership

We are already observing shifts in association culture relating to leadership. In the traditional association, great pride is taken in making good decisions. In the knowledge-based association, leadership knows the limits of its expertise and takes pride in seeing that a good decision is made.

Manipulating Versus Leadership

In the traditional association, information is distributed selectively to bring attention to what is important—attention is managed. Information is selectively distributed to get certain groups to appreciate the value of what you are proposing and to earn the trust of groups who are needed to give support to initiatives. You do not tell things that might bother people whose support you need. This behavior is incompatible with a knowledge-based culture.

This critical distinction involves an inherent difference between leadership and manipulation. Leadership in an association is achieved by influencing the behavior of others. Both leadership and manipulation, however, are based on how information—the leader's primary currency—is used.

Imagine for a moment that you are a member. Your leader is trying to get you to believe something or do something he honestly believes is in your best interest. If that leader was going to manipulate you, he would not share with you complete information or his true intentions if he thought you would believe or behave differently than he wanted you to as a result.

Manipulation is not a sustainable leadership strategy. In most associations, a secret should be defined as something you tell one person at a time. Once the secret is out you will be called on it. Once you are called on it, trust will not likely be extended again.

Leaders in a knowledge-based enterprise, on the other hand, use information in different phases to accomplish different things. First, they use information to develop understanding of what it is they are proposing and of what value it would be to members. Then they use information to help identify alternative strategies that might be used to reach the goal and to select a strategy. In addition, they use it to measure progress being made and to celebrate success along the way. Further, they use information to evaluate and appreciate what they have done, and, finally, they repeat the cycle to see what has to happen next. If leaders are using information that way, they are leading by using the information to influence members' perceptions that result in behavior.

The distinction between manipulation and leadership is critical. It reflects difference in values held in the knowledge-based culture and the traditional culture.

Leaders Shape Culture

The chief staff officer leads the staff organization's culture, and the chief elected officer leads culture on the volunteer side. The two of them, collectively, best lead the whole organization.

As a leadership team, there are some ways they can create, change, or at least affect culture. One leverage point affecting an organization's culture is what leaders pay attention to and how much attention they give. The rest of the organization is out there watching the two leaders in the spotlight. To the degree leaders pay attention to certain things, the membership gives those things importance. What and how leaders communicate provides another leverage point influencing how members view the culture of the organization. This includes not only what and how they communicate verbally, but also how the leaders behave in highly visible situations.

Besides leadership enabling mechanisms, there exist organizational enabling mechanisms. These include structure, policy, procedures, and bylaws. They represent the structural elements and key processes through which information is exchanged and decisions are made.

Build on Existing Foundations

Most associations already have in place a greater foundation to build on for becoming knowledge based than they think. Review the status, characteristics, and culture of your association. The odds are high that you will find a good foundation in place.

Examine your pluses; those are the places to build from. Look at where complacency has promoted inertia; those are places to improve. Look at your minuses and, unless they represent extraordinarily difficult challenges or are extremely important strategically, remedy them in a later phase of your journey. These elements represent a template leadership can use to prioritize areas needing attention.

How these are attended to will differ from organization to organization. The need to pay attention to them, however, and to determine how effectively you are doing this will be critical for leading associations into the twenty-first century.

How do you know that taking this journey will be worth the effort for the organization? This journey is well worth considering if your association wishes to improve its ability to accomplish any of the following:

- to create new products or services quickly in response to fast-developing, changing markets
- to experiment constantly
- to change organizational structures in response to market changes
- to use well-informed, self-managed teams in decision making and consensus building

One of the important values of the knowledge-based operational philosophy is the comfortable environment it creates for consultative relationships. The existence of consultative relationships enables the execution of critical competencies in an effective fashion.

New Ways to Access Benefits

Most associations, in the past, have been in the business of either sending things to people as benefits or having people go somewhere to get them. The historic measure of success in many associations has been the "count" of how many people attend a meeting and how many people read the journal.

Now, however, associations are moving into business lines and programming where benefits are accessed differently. The number of people attending your annual meeting may become a less useful measure of success in the future, particularly if members are accessing learning opportunities on line. The future measure of success might be hit rates or visitors on the Internet.

Associations today find a lot of competitors for what they have been doing in the past. There are some things associations will never be strategically well positioned to do. It is unlikely that any association will enjoy long-term success as a source of leading-edge technology to access knowledge, insight, and information. Most do not have the intellectual capital to accomplish this, and, even if they did, it is not likely they have the technical expertise. Most wise associations look for outside partners for joint ventures to provide access to learning and insight through such a medium.

Sources of Knowledge

Associations have usually been particularly good at one thing. Most associations enjoy strong competitive advantages in being (1) sources of knowledge, not just information, and (2) sources of insight, not just ideas, related to issues important to the professions or industries they serve. While they may not be the best medium through which information is accessed, if they handle things right, they can sustain their positions as primary sources of accessible knowledge or insight.

Your private partner vendor brings the pipe through which information can pass. You bring good content for the pipe. That is what is meant by recognizing the value of and continuously cultivating the intellectual assets of your organization. If you lose your position as the source of the most useful knowledge, then you have lost a strategic advantage central to your future success.

There is an important distinction between information and knowledge. If someone gives you data and a description of something, you are receiving information. That is not difficult, and people do it all the time. But if someone

1. gives you data,
2. gives a description of information,
3. tells you why that data is important to you,

4. helps you understand what parts of it are most important,
5. gives you advice on how to use it, and
6. counsels you on what you might expect to happen if you use it in certain ways,

that source has moved from being a purveyor of information to being a pool of access to knowledge.

Your membership wants you to be a source of knowledge, not just a distributor of information. Your intellectual capital allows you to be the source of knowledge.

There exists another level where intellectual capital can be used beyond knowledge. If someone gave you information, knowledge, and advice on what to do and how to do it, and that person also had enough experience to say, "Listen, if you try this, here's what you can expect to happen," that person just moved to the level of wisdom.

Significant Change Area Three: What Gets Rewarded

Another area where significant change is visible is in what gets rewarded. The traditional association places value in people who do a lot of work. The knowledge-based association places value in people who are able to achieve results.

As time goes on, the most talented members of your profession will be less and less able to give their time for activity. You will need to develop ways to access the energy and insight they can provide that allow you to achieve the right outcomes.

In the traditional association's culture, members pay dues in the organization, put in time to move ahead, and then are chosen to participate. Politically correct work and leader groups are based on the amount of time people have dedicated to the organization. This rewards loyalty, not insight, intelligence, and contribution.

The knowledge-based association still pays attention to that, but also rewards people who exhibit certain personal and professional competencies as they execute what they have been asked to do. It seeks leaders who can think critically, extrapolate, and analyze. People are chosen to participate in issues on the basis of their abilities more than on the basis of whether or not they have paid their dues.

The reward system determines the character of people who will be attracted to work and decision groups. The collective ability of these human resources will also influence the extent to which essential competencies will be executed effectively.

Significant Change Area Four: Managing Intellectual Capital

The authors of "Managing Intellectual Assets," in a review published in *Fortune* (October 3, 1994) identify two types of knowledge—rules-based (bylaws, procedures, etc.) and wisdom, experience, and stories. The implications of this insight for the next seventy-five years of association evolution are enormous. First, failure to properly manage knowledge assets:

1. increases vulnerability;
2. is often part of what occurs when moving from the early stages to mature stages of the organization (what the authors of "Managing Intellectual Assets" called "losing the recipe");
3. breaks an important link with the past that would increase effectiveness while managing through change; and
4. results in an organization comprised of "islands of knowledge."

Second, many organizations need to reconsider traditional practices that keep the same people in the same position (staff and member volunteers), rather than continually developing, supporting, and growing knowledge assets. Third, critical processes in the organization—such as needs assessment, strategic planning, policy development, and budgeting—need to be reshaped, not just re-engineered. The objective will be to increase value, not merely to reduce costs.

Fourth, when effectively used, development of knowledge needs to become as much of an individual as an organizational responsibility. Maintaining and growing competencies individuals in the organization need for their positions becomes as much the individuals' responsibilities as the organization's. The individual must assume responsibility for finding out what they are supposed to know that they do not know. This is often best done through books, asking people, shadowing colleagues, and accessing outside courses and networks of experience, rather than through training, which frequently, is many organizations' inefficient contribution to continuing professional development.

Integrating Technology

Among the most frequently mentioned challenges associations face related to building a knowledge-based culture is choosing from the tidal wave of available new technologies. From the Internet and the rapid rush to on-line delivery of member services, to using video conferencing to enhance face-to-face meetings, to the quandary of what to do about association management software programs, association executives face constant questions. These relate to how much technology to implement, how to most effectively integrate it into an association's work processes, and how to use it effectively as a tool to achieve a knowledge-based culture.

Using technology effectively is a critical factor in building a knowledge-based culture. It is also a core capability of twenty-first century organizations. Technology, when effectively integrated into association work processes, can enable the collection, dissemination, and processing of information. Technology enables the shift from data to information to knowledge. There are challenges inherent in making those shifts: how does an association effectively turn data into information and knowledge? The short answer is by sharing it across functional and process areas within the organization.

What is Typical?

Consider a typical association. The membership database system technology is DOS, character-based, was internally developed, and handles basic functionality like membership information, dues payments, and perhaps meeting and educational program attendance. The membership services department is the "keeper" of this data, and, in some cases, is the only department that possesses either access to the system or the skill required to access it. It may also be responsible for membership needs assessment. The results of those activities may be contained in reports and surveys in hard copy format, but are not integrated into the database.

The meetings department has its own database of exhibitors and registration information, which is not tied into the membership system. The education department keeps course evaluations and registrations and some sort of demographic data collected through attendance at seminars, but this information is not captured in the membership database. The finance department is on a separate general ledger system.

The publications department has been given responsibility for launching a web site and keeping its content up-to-date. It does not, however, have access to either the content information kept in other departments or statistics about what members are interested in learning. Alternately, the director has been given responsibility for the web site and spends most of his or her time canvassing department heads to find out what members want to know from the association that could be put on the web site.

What is wrong with this picture? Data, data everywhere—but no effective system with which to use it to create knowledge. In the above description, there exists:

1. A lack of a process and technical infrastructure to collect and allow access to knowledge about members across the organization

2. Segmented membership data—each piece is owned by a function, and the association staff is not structured to allow optimum information sharing and knowledge creation

The challenge of effectively integrating information across an association's staff and volunteer work structure and processes, and the ability for associations to be able to turn data into value-added information and knowledge are some of the most significant issues in becoming knowledge based. Critical information about member demographics, preferences, and behavior are essential to usefully exchanging information and insights in a knowledge-based decision process. The competencies are essential; the culture enables their effective use in design, development, and decision processes.

Efficient, Coherent Key Processes

Knowledge-based associations carefully and continually assess the efficiency and coherency of the key processes that must be informed by such data. Efficiency refers to ease of access to data as well as its timeliness and accuracy. Coherency refers to the ability to extract and merge information from across databases. In most associations, effective design and use of these key processes has as much to do with the quality of decisions as does the quality of the information itself.

In a knowledge-based organization, these key processes are routinely assessed to determine whether and to what extent they are providing the organization the judgments needed for successful policy, program, and operational decisions. These key processes are the vehicles through which necessary information and insight is exchanged between people and places that possess knowledge. These people include decision makers, developers, and program implementers in each of the five other elements of an association infrastructure discussed in detail earlier in this text.

In knowledge-based associations, the processes of the organization through which decisions are made and carried out are likely to be as important as the structures through which people and their functional responsibilities are organized. Associations that maintain successful processes frequently subject them to purposeful evaluation. While a variety of approaches can be employed, process evaluation in a knowledge-based environment must include examination of the following questions. These consider factors of cost, quality, speed, and member satisfaction. Factors are analyzed based on current strengths, gaps, and new process requirements.

1. Where would improvements in cost, quality, speed, or member satisfaction provide the greatest service advantage?

Typical Association Processes

1. ***Needs Assessment Process***—continuous, systematic process for collecting, analyzing, interpreting, and providing defensible information about (1) member needs, expectations, experiences and preferences; (2) capacity and strategic position of the organization; (3) evolving dynamics of environments related to members

2. ***Strategic Planning Process***—including (1) development of vision, mission, goals, strategies, and resource allocation; (2) fiscal strategies; (3) annual budget related to plan; and (4) monitoring of the plan and adjustment as needed

3. ***Policy Process***—the decision-making system linking the strategic plan, emerging issues, and committee assignments that includes (1) positions policy issues; (2) positions on operational issues taken on the basis of executive committee, committee, task force, and/or staff analysis; and (3) documentation of external and internal policy decisions

4. ***Program Development/Support***—processes of staff and volunteers; may explore each major program area, for example, education, government relations, legal, and others

5. ***Meeting Support***—including annual meeting and all other meetings

6. ***Membership***—recruitment, retention and processing of all membership-related activities, including dues payment

7. ***Human Resources Management***—including recruitment, retention, personnel policy development, employee benefits, reporting relationships and responsibilities

8. ***Staff Support***—processes to support various organizational structures within the association such as board, councils, committees, and related organizations

9. ***Member Communications***—communication/information flows with members

10. ***External Communications***—with key stakeholder groups

11. ***Internal Communications***—communications and reporting among staff, the board, committees, and other organizational units; types of communications involved, processes used, effectiveness, appropriate use of technology, cost-benefit analysis of current procedures

12. ***Management Information***—processes supporting association, staff and members, hardware and software use, as well as application of special technologies like desktop publishing, Internet communications, and others

13. ***Administrative/Management Functions***—processes supporting management of the association

2. How can the association leverage what it does well to satisfy the requirements of members and capitalize on new opportunities to serve members?
3. What process gaps exist between what the association is promising its members today and the associations' actual performance?
4. Which process gaps must be closed to avoid eroding the association's membership base?
5. What new process requirements must the association meet to satisfy emerging needs?
6. What new processes must the association design to be able to develop new programs and satisfy the unstated future needs of current and future members?
7. What is the association unable to do today, that if it was able, would give the association a great advantage over others seeking to serve its members?

You are What You Eat

A particularly salient example of the interaction of organizational competencies and a culture that will either support or prevent effective execution is found in ways an organization handles technology and information management. The old data processing bromide of "garbage in . . . garbage out" has been replaced by a newer analogy more suited to information management—"You are what you eat."

Just as the human system converts food to nutrients that fuel the organism, in a knowledge-based association data is converted to knowledge that fuels the enterprise. This organic metaphor suggests three new rules for using information management technologies in an association seeking to be knowledge based.

Rule number one: Eat too little and risk wasting away. Technology provides tools for exchanging information and insight. If the exchange is insufficiently, erroneously, or irrelevantly informed, the organization risks wasting away due to poor "nutrients" feeding its decision making processes.

Rule number two: Eat too much and risk being unable to move quickly. Because technology provides for the exchange of information and insight, if the processes for exchange are overloaded with useless or unfocused information, then, like any organism that is overfed with non-nutritious food, it becomes bloated and unable to move with any degree of efficiency or nimbleness. The same tenet applies to selecting and using technology. Technology without clear purpose or real use inhibits efficiency.

Rule number three: "What you eat is more important than how much." Technology should not just increase efficiency, it should also add value. Knowledge-based organizations identify, select, and implement technology with the equally important objectives of increasing efficiency, effectiveness, and value.

In associations the two basic purposes for technology applications are member/market data management and communications. Some of the technology uses for member/market data management include general association management and customer/member services. Some of the increasingly common uses of technology for communications include providing customized access to polls of information, knowledge, and supporting group work being conducted at different times or places.

Four technology-related issues confront association executives managing migration to a more knowledge-based operational philosophy.

1. *What is the appropriate mix between demand and capacity?*

   When less than half the membership has the capability, confidence, and competence to take advantage of a technology-assisted service, does the association postpone development and installation or does it proceed ahead of its member market? In the knowledge-based enterprise, the association should proceed in developing its necessary competencies, so that when the majority of membership "catches up," the association will not be vulnerable to being replaced as a source of the member service by another organization or place that moved ahead.

2. *What or who will drive demand?*

   It is likely that associations will continue to see demand for improved uses of technology for communications and information management coming from members who are using these technologies in work and at home. If these users tend to be the leading-edge thinkers of the organization, its most influential members, or its most potent internal pace setters, then the association should take advantage of their status with their colleagues. The association should garner their support to complete the associations' "learning curve" as quickly and expertly as possible.

3. *What will need to change about the organization?*

   Depending on the improvement technology is being employed to support, the association may need to adjust any or all of its processes to realize the full potential of the tool selected. Structures, processes, staff competencies, systems, and paradigms for decision-making and involvement may all need to be reinvented or reshaped. Simply using a new technology to execute an old work process seldom allows an organization to fully enjoy the benefits of what can be a significant investment. The knowledge-based organization approaches technology decisions by first determining improvement desired, then determining whether technology can support the improvement. If the answer to the latter is yes, then the association will select the most appropriate technology with full understanding and commitment to all that is required for successful implementation and continued use.

4. *Where should we start?*

   Associations following the basic logic suggested above start where improvement of efficiency and added value will be transparent and achievable. Effectively using technology in an organization involves an incremental rather than a revolutionary strategy. Technology is seldom the obstacle to full benefit. Usually the greatest obstacle is changing perceptions among users and potential beneficiaries. They need to be convinced that the new work process has sufficient value to warrant the energy that converting old habits to new practices involves.

Technology used by members drives demand on associations. As technology use becomes more pervasive in organizations and industries, more pressure will be placed on associations to use the same types of communication with members, like fax, Internet, groupware, and video conferencing.

Consider the implications of new-found or dramatically enhanced competency in technology and information management on the historic culture of the organization. The shift to a technology-enabled work environment also facilitates the move from a political to a knowledge-based model of decision making and from managing change incrementally to a philosophy of managing through change.

Associations must start with the lowest common technology. Find out where members are on the technology learning curve, and build a migration strategy of technology use sophisticated enough to satisfy your leading-edge "pioneer" members, flexible enough to meet needs of middle-of-the-road technology "settlers," but basic enough to encourage and bring along the technology "stragglers."

Build a strategy of incremental change—use a parallel strategy of migrating products and services from paper-based to electronic delivery. Finally, build an evolving vision of how technology will enable a culture of knowledge-based decision making in your association. Consider how the necessary commitments to innovation and risk taking will likely infiltrate other competencies of the organization once they become imbedded in its culture.

CHAPTER 13

Toward Virtual Organizations

The local chapter of ABC association is holding its monthly dinner meeting. Turnout is good, networking is strong, and the discussion and ideas are flowing. The speaker is well received by the group, and the meeting evaluation forms reflect a high level of member satisfaction.

This "dinner" session was held not in one conference site, but in the kitchens and dens of hundreds of members. The discussion was held "virtually," through an on-line chat forum hosted through the association's web site. Member networking, information transfer, and group discussion all occurred through technology-assisted means, and member satisfaction, commitment, and involvement in the association's activities is reaching an all-time high.

The board of ABC association is holding its quarterly meeting. An agenda has been distributed, discussion has begun, and the group is facing a critical decision.

While some board members are physically attending, others are networked into the meeting from remote locations, through their computers. At the front of the meeting room, a facilitator is equipped with a video projector, an electronic whiteboard, and laptop computer. Board members are seated around a u-shaped table, equipped with networked laptop computers. When decisions need to be made, participants can vote their convictions (anonymously if desired) using group decision software. The facilitator and the technology keep the meeting focused, participants quickly and efficiently conclude their business, decisions and action item data are available immediately, and all leave with the sense that much has been accomplished.

The Shift

A shift has begun. Responding to competitive pressures, the organizational model is changing, not simply to a new static model, but to a dynamic, fluid model. In many organizations, TQM, rightsizing, and business process re-engineering initiatives are evidence of this shift. Everyone is looking to find the right structure—when in reality, perhaps the right structure is more like an amoebae—fluid, adaptable, and dynamic.

Organizations of all kinds are developing new ways to structure work. Many have already begun to implement new strategic imperatives; to restructure their organizations for dynamic, interdisciplinary teams; to strive to respond more effectively to member needs by embracing "customer intimacy;" all while attempting to anticipate the constantly changing competitive environments they now face.

These are primary attributes of knowledge-based systems, structures, and processes supported by what is valued in a knowledge-based culture.

The scenarios above represent a fundamental shift in the nature of association business—both in member services and in staff/governance activities. While most associations have undoubtedly begun to experience a pull toward integrating technology into their work processes, and many have begun to experiment with technology-assisted organization processes, a clear direction has been slow to emerge. This is clouded by the high cost of many technologies, the hype of competing platforms, and conflicting pressures from members.

Despite these startup woes, associations have begun to move toward becoming "virtual" organizations. They must accelerate their efforts to effectively compete with non-traditional sources of education, involvement, advocacy, and community in the coming digital economy.

There are many competitive advantages inherent in the traditional association organizational structure. In a very real sense, associations have been virtual organizations for the past 150 years. With staff functions, members, and boards disbursed often over vast geographic and physical locales, associations have effectively functioned for years without the benefit of their entire leadership or member and staff populations housed in contiguous physical surroundings. Still they have learned to collaborate, communicate, and deliberate effectively. This has not always been the case for private sector organizations, where regional management has often suffered from being "away from headquarters."

The Virtual Environment

With enabling technology now on the threshold of critical mass, the concept of "virtual work," or the "virtual organization," has moved toward becoming attainable and realistic. Given the predisposition inherent in association organizational structures, how can associations most effectively and expediently embrace this new paradigm? What are the implications of this trend for the future of associations? What is virtual work? Why is it critical to the future of associations? How can associations benefit from implementing prototypes of future work processes?

We will look at five major components of the virtual environment:

1. the shift to virtual,
2. the need for collaboration,
3. embracing knowledge-based fundamentals,

4. a focus on continuous organizational learning, and
5. the use of enabling virtual technologies.

In just a few short years, the year 2000 will be here. The post-millennium era will undoubtedly see more organizations integrate multi-location work with new ways of conducting collaborative work, in both electronic and physical spaces. This shift will redefine today's business environment altogether. The model is changing rapidly.

Time and space are being redefined. Shifts are occurring on several levels—geographic, with the evolving global environment; physical, with little need for physical "headquarters" sites any longer; and electronic, with the anytime, anywhere office.

Don Tapscott (1996) has articulated this shift and has identified several new "drivers for success," including *knowledge*, which identifies the need to not only manage information but to create new forms of collaborative intellect; *digitization*, which speaks to the technological enhancements of information flow; and *virtualization*, which focuses on redefining time and space.

The Shift to Virtual

Among the most pervasive of these trends, and among the most critical to associations, is *virtualization*. Virtuality has arrived. The concept of "virtuality" is beginning to permeate our business lives. The move is from analog to digital, and from physical to virtual. There are now virtual ballot boxes, government agencies, villages and communities, malls, corporations, jobs, and teams.

Too, there are now evolving "virtual organizations." Remember Steve Case's quote:

> Our members have told us they want access to a broad range of content, presented in an engaging way, easy-to-use, affordably priced, and with a strong sense of community. These factors are the underpinnings of our success, because our members have, in turn, brought other members . . .

America On-Line, itself an example of the consequences to an organization of dramatic industry change, can actually be considered not just an on-line community, but a "virtual association," representing a very non-traditional, yet significant, competitive threat to many associations, with its advocacy, education, and other member services.

Why have these trends emerged at this point? Several elements have recently converged, including the global nature of the evolving business environment, the growing scarcity and geographic disparity of worker knowledge due to restructuring and down sizing, and the general availability, cost reduction, and standardization of enabling technologies in the areas of communications and computing.

As both member and staff organizations flatten and restructure, resources become more and more scarce. In increasingly fluid environments, it becomes more difficult (and often more expensive—in terms of both time and money), to bring people together to set policy, guide programs, and make critical decisions.

Communications and computer technologies are beginning to offer the tools to navigate this constantly changing environment. Association leaders will be able to work together from their homes and offices almost as easily as if they were in the same physical location. Although separated by space and often by time, they will be able to share and review information, collaborate with other colleagues, and make effective decisions together.

The Need for Collaboration

The key to success in the new virtual world is constructing a collaborative environment where people can work effectively in mutual endeavors, cooperate, learn, and make decisions together. Collaboration in associations, whether within work groups, between remote sites, or between association leadership, members, and staff, is becoming the new model for success.

We would define a collaborative association structure as one possessing these attributes:

- Everyone has access to the right information, within the right context, at the right time, in the right place
- Teams are the basic building blocks of the organization
- Information can flow within and between organizations
- The organization, its systems, and its structures, are dynamic
- The organization has moved toward becoming knowledge based

Embracing Knowledge-Based Fundamentals

Associations by nature are collaborative, and those that are moving toward being knowledge based manifest these tendencies particularly. The essentials of becoming knowledge based include a focus on information sharing, team-based structures, enabling technologies, flexible organizations, and a high-involvement culture.

To create a fully collaborative environment, we add one more essential to those of becoming knowledge based, borrowing from the work of Peter Senge. Senge's seminal work, *The Fifth Discipline* (1990), describes a focus on continuous learning as having these organizational effects:

- Continuously improves an organization by anticipating and creating skills needed for future success (the ability to thrive on change)
- Maximizes learning opportunities by nurturing and tapping the collective wisdom of its entire staff
- Establishes a setting where people are constantly and spontaneously learning and applying their knowledge
- Creates an environment where learning is valued as perhaps the most critical source of competitive advantage and where learning has become synonymous with working

The shift from a physical to a virtual environment is at once an impediment and a driver toward continuous learning. As more and more work is done independent of a common physical and spatial environment, it becomes a larger challenge to sustain effective levels of creativity, free information flow, and spontaneous learning opportunities inherent in face-to-face sessions. Over time, groups may experience a loss of community due to the isolating nature of technology.

Through the use of collaborative computing and groupware systems, the process of knowledge creation can be dramatically accelerated. Senge refers to a concept known as "team learning," which he describes as one "driven by common needs, common problems, a quest for new knowledge, and the desire to collaborate." Whether it is manifested in the sharing of best practices or organizational "memory" data, when properly facilitated, on-line collaboration enables bringing together the best ideas, creation of new knowledge, and maintenance of a constant focus on continuous learning. Technology's greatest potential in the collaborative organization is not its ability to disseminate existing information, but rather, its potential to facilitate the creation, capture, and sharing of new knowledge in a collaborative context.

The drive to collaborate cannot be overemphasized. There must be a very compelling, real reason for association staff and members to collaborate with technology as a tool. A hope that the novelty of the knowledge will be a sufficient driver for use—absent some real work that must be done that someone is accountable for—is likely to be a false and very disappointed hope.

Enabling Technologies

The infrastructure that will enable work to be accomplished more effectively, and in an environment of knowledge-based decision making and continuous organizational learning, can be collectively referred to as "virtual technology."

As we trace the trends of the past twenty years, technology has evolved from mainframe to personal computing, toward the rapid approach of interpersonal computing. Applications have moved from merely functionally based, like accounting, customer service, and human resources, to cross-functional process, and finally toward the accumulation of collective knowledge and intelligence.

The evolution of collaborative computing began in the early 1970s and 1980s. Moving from simple messaging, to bulletin board, to computer conferencing, computing began to be free of space/time dependence.

Today, with the rapid advent of the Internet and other network-based architectures, our information environments are moving from computer centric to network centric. With all of the rapid developments, it would be easy to shift technology's role from that of tool to driver. But we must resist the tendency to do so. The issue is not one of which technology is the best, but when to use the right technology. Remember, technology must serve as an *enabler*—not a *driver*. The pressures inherent on associations today to implement a myriad of new technologies in a rapid period of time are immense. So are the dangers if the association has not integrated strategic goals and objectives into the mixture.

If an association's goals are clearly in sight, using virtual technology can have enormous, positive organizational benefits. While technology obviously offers a great many technical enhancements in association organizational efficiency, it is the possibility of transforming organizational behavior that has the greatest potential.

Groupware

Groupware is the vector of electronic communication, information management, and group focus. The enabling technologies collectively known as groupware are information systems designed to enable groups to work together electronically. There are three critical elements to any groupware system: electronic communication, database of group knowledge, and support for group activity.

Groupware can make associations more productive by (1) removing the barriers of time and space, (2) creating common forums for discussion and information exchange, (3) establishing a place for shared data, and (4) providing tools for dealing effectively with a large amount of heterogeneous data. Categories of groupware applications include: electronic mail/messaging, calendaring and scheduling systems, group document handling, group decision systems and meeting support, and information sharing and video conferencing products.

Many associations have already begun to see some of the benefits of virtual work through implementation of groupware tools like e-mail, Internet web sites, Intranets, news groups, bulletin boards, video conferencing, and various document conferencing systems.

One of the most exciting developments for associations is the advent of collaborative computing—the combination of desktop video and shared applications. Through using these technologies, virtual team members can view the same application at the same time, as well as view their colleagues—wherever they are.

By using collaborative tools like remote pointers, highlighters, writing tools, private workspaces, drawing tools, and application sharing, virtual teams are often more able to function effectively virtually than they do when working face-to-face. Among the obvious benefits of these technologies are: fewer face-to-face meetings, shorter meetings, decreased travel time, less time spent waiting for responses, faster information transmission and retrieval, greater individual control over interruptions, faster decision making, and improved organizational learning.

Groupware meeting enhancement capabilities can be particularly effective tools for associations. In a groupware meeting, an agenda, list of questions, or proposal is posted in a forum before the meeting. Everyone can preview the materials, post comments, and respond to comments when it is convenient for them. Strategic planning sessions and board and committee work can be accelerated substantially. Everyone can come to face-to-face sessions with a clear understanding of the background issues, and precious face-to-face meeting time can be reserved for true collaborative discussion and decision making.

By holding meetings this way, the association's organizational "memory" grows, creating automatic "minutes" that help new staff and members understand the association or issue history, which can be useful in analyzing past practice and lessons learned. New staff and volunteers can get up to speed quickly and easily. Everyone can access a central repository of group knowledge. To the knowledge-based enterprise, this means greater depth and breadth and easier access to the intellectual capital of the association. This is likely to be one of its primary competitive advantages into the twenty-first century.

Moving Forward to Virtual—Lessons Learned

As we have seen, both in the association community and the private sector, the shift to virtual has begun. Pilot applications have been identified and implemented, and there already exists a small base of empirical results.

Most early adopters have focused primarily on the technology, and, until now, little attention has been paid to organizational issues. Understanding and implementing the technology is not enough. Virtual work involves fundamental shifts in the way people work together—in the way they communicate and collaborate.

Groupware divides into two words—*group* and *ware*. Most of the initial focus has been on the "ware" side. Technology implementation without the proper "team orientation" can be counter productive. In groupware or conferencing implementation, for example, we often forget these critical additions: calendar and reservations, electronic meeting training, and audio-conference backup capabilities. Large group meetings may need technographers, virtual on-line facilitators, and more effective pre-meeting work planning. Most critically, organizational processes may need to be redesigned to accommodate the aspects of virtual work.

Several components of being knowledge based and the new world of virtual work have been discussed here: the shift to virtual, the need to collaborate, a focus on continuous learning, and the implementation of enabling technologies. The bottom line, however, starts and ends with people. Organizations leverage knowledge through networks of people who collaborate—not through networks of technology that interconnect. Technologies are merely enablers. The work of the association and its members are the real drivers.

While the pace of technology may drive us to change, in the end, it is us—people—who must change. New, virtual work methods mean fundamental changes in the way people work on a daily basis.

The shift to virtual has already begun elsewhere. Some of today's small, successful high-technology companies have distilled their entire mission statements down to three words: "Get Bigger Faster." Associations will be competitive in the new virtual environment only if they can learn faster than either their current or emerging competitors. In the race to the virtual finish line, lifelong organizational learning will become the only sustainable competitive advantage. It is suggested here that, as leading-edge associations position for success in the new virtual world, their missions should be to "Get Smarter Faster."

The Internet—Hype or Help?

Tucked in an article in *Business Week* about Microsoft's Internet strategies against Netscape was this quote:

> Microsoft, already the ultimate hard-core company, is entering a new dimension. It's called Internet Time: a pace so frenetic it's like living dog years—each jammed with the events of seven normal ones (July 15, 1996).

There is no doubt. The Internet has grown exponentially in recent years. The pace of growth, along with the nature of the technology itself, has sped up both the amount of information being thrown at us, and the changes in the ways it is delivered.

For many associations, this new environment has meant new pressures from members to jump on the Net bandwagon and to establish web sites, and indeed, most associations have either already brought up their home pages or have plans to do so. Unfortunately, however, the move is usually reactive rather than proactive.

Many associations with well-established web sites are just now trying to develop strategies and purposes for being on line! Others are already re-engineering their sites. Still others have concluded that their web site is a process—not a site or a product—and have begun to treat its maintenance as a function of the organization like its lobbying activities, policy process, or telephone-based consultation to members. No matter which way an association chooses to regard its web site, it should consider several key factors in its design:

1. *Define your objectives*—What do you hope to achieve with a web site? How do you expect it to be used?
2. *Define your target audiences*—Who are most likely visitors, and what will they want to get from the site?
3. *Define content information*—Based on the objectives and information needs of target audiences, what are the core information areas that should make up the web site?
4. *Define potential competition*—Based on what you know about your members' interests, what competitive web sites might exist, and will the target audience compare them? If so, how will you draw the audience to your site?
5. *Establish links*—What other sites should be linked to yours? A state or national site? ASAE or others? Should you register with search engines such as Alta Vista and Yahoo?

6. *Plan marketing and publicity*—How should the word get out about your site?

Although there is certainly a need to keep content new and fresh, this constant activity suggests that associations have not yet hit on the most effective or even an acceptable use of on-line services. So why establish Web presence? The potential for enhanced member services represents a fundamental shift in the nature of delivery methodologies that associations will use to communicate.

The Internet, like the wave of other technologies sweeping through associations, can be seen as a two-edged sword. On one hand, it enables competitors—both traditional and non-traditional—to more easily attract and serve your members. On the other hand, it opens up many new vehicles for associations to serve their members more effectively.

CHAPTER 14

Repositioning the Organization

Associations can be very static. They tend to resist change. They tend to build up, balancing crisis, friction, and problems until they reach a point where they break. Fortunately, most of the time they do not break; they change without realizing it. As a consequence of this, traditional associations tend to improve in surges.

The knowledge-based association is better positioned to sustain ongoing improvement. In such an environment the political trauma is likely to be lessened, and energy can be directed to implementing change rather than surviving it. The new knowledge-based model allows associations to get ahead of the change curve, to start moving before they must.

Diagnostic Keys

There are a number of diagnostic keys that can be used to consider whether you should think seriously about re-positioning your association.

Crisis Keys

The crisis keys are used when you are on a ship, about to hit a lighthouse out of light bulbs. You have got to find and install some light bulbs quickly so the ship does not get on the rocks or hit the lighthouse. Three fairly severe conditions necessitate using crisis keys. These conditions suggest need for re-engineering. The degree and pace of change required will be dictated by the particular circumstances.

Crisis One: Key Members Abandon

The first condition is when key members abandon the association and, in some cases, even become competitors. There are a variety of reasons for this, and it is probably the greatest internal crisis that occurs in many associations.

First, it is caused by differences over policy. Here is an example revealing the importance of external affairs review. Several years ago, Citicorp Mortgage Company, the largest member of the National Association of Realtors, a trade association composed of agents, brokers, appraisers, and other participants in the real estate industry, came up with a system that bypassed the organization's usual delivery system for a particular service.

Citicorp's system allowed direct electronic contact between a borrower and the ultimate lender. It bypassed brokers who, traditionally, had been part of the process. This clearly varied with the trade association's policies, and it had a major affect on the trade association.

At that point, the association and its largest member became competitors. Ultimately, however, the problem was resolved when Citicorp encountered a number of technical problems rendering the system basically inefficient. Significantly, though, by that time, a difference over policy had been created that was a major problem for the association.

A second reason members leave is because of perceived or actual lack of service. They do not care about things the executive officer does; they are more concerned with matters that hit close to home.

The National Association of Realtors had an affiliate that left because it perceived a lack of service by the parent organization. This appraisers' organization thought the

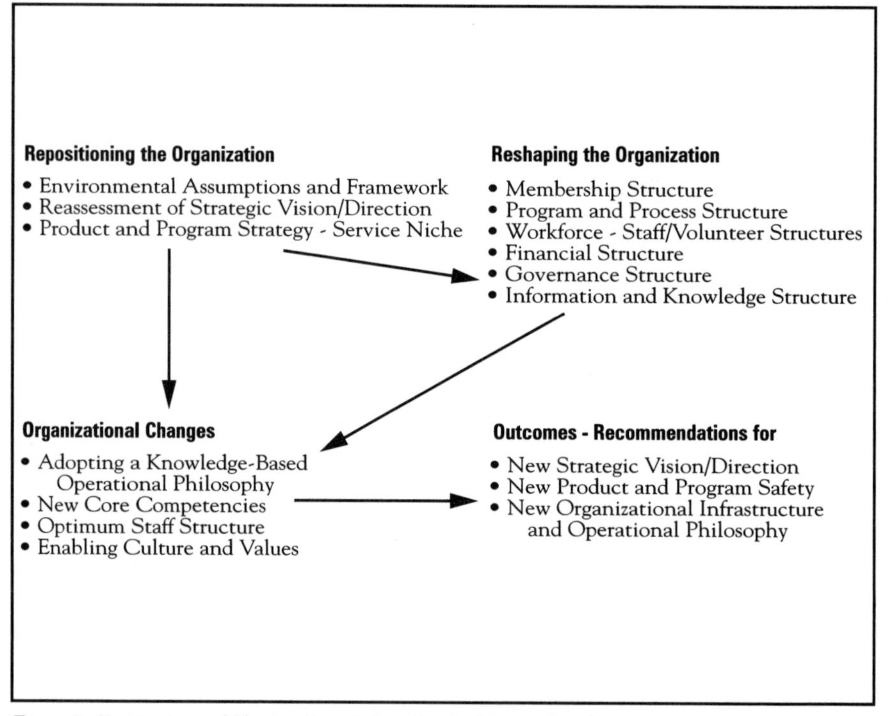

Figure 8. Positioning and Shaping Associations for the Twenty-first Century

national organization cared only about residential brokers for quotes on home values. While not the case, this was the perception. That kind of discontinuity, when a major member segment perceives its interests are not being served, causes another crisis.

Key members also abandon the association due to inability to affect governance. Typical expressions are, "I represent 10 percent of the industry, why do I only have one seat on the board of directors?" "Why am I not on the board of directors?" "Why can't I influence policy? If I can't do that, and I'm as big as I am, I'm going to get up and walk out. I'm going to leave the association and become a competitor."

Again, using the real estate industry as an example, a large brokerage firm that does not have the say it wants in the local organization decides to get up and leave. It starts a competitive real estate information system and a competitive multiple listing service. Suddenly a key member is outside the tent, and a problem exists. That first crisis when key members abandon the association can come in a variety of ways and for a variety of reasons. It is a very strong internal signal that something is going wrong, and a look at re-engineering may be in order.

Crisis Two: Technological Change

A second important external crisis key is technological change. Technology can change in a way threatening to the industry and the association. It can strongly suggest that changing the makeup and operation of the association may be necessary because major industry products are no longer desired. A good example is the record industry. In 1984, 43 percent of production for the recording industry was done on vinyl records; in 1993, this was 1 percent. Technology caused changes in the marketplace wiping out an entire product. Wiping out that product forced a change in the interests of that industry.

Changes in technology can significantly alter an industry's delivery system as well. College book stores have changed, for example. What do you do when you no longer have a print version of a book because it is on compact disc?

Crisis Three: Regulatory, Legislative, or Economic Changes

The third external crisis key is represented by regulatory, legislative, or economic changes that can cause extraordinary alteration in an industry and even destroy it. Here there are really two subsectors. Major legal changes are always direct—these are things like tax changes. The Tax Act of 1986, for example, wiped out the entire syndication industry and eliminated limited partnerships.

Regulatory, legislative, or economic changes also result in industries becoming smaller or larger. For example, the number of banking industry thrift institutions in 1980 was twice what it is today. At that time there were a number of state associations, and now there is only one.

Discomfort Keys

A lot of associations are currently going through major changes triggering the need for re-engineering. It pays to look back on your own association to see where these things might apply.

Some conditions are not necessarily crises. They are not things that stare at you in the face and jump out and hit you; they are more subtle. These are "discomfort keys." They represent the beginning of something, but you are not quite sure what. They are uncertain, but they may be making you uneasy.

Discomfort One: Inability to Predict the Future

At the top of the list of the discomfort keys is the inability to predict where an industry will be in five years. What is coming down the pike? What is the shape of the industry going to be? What is the relative size and education of the membership going to be? What are the needs of that industry going to be? There are a number of industries currently beginning that five-year change, and they simply cannot predict what they are going to look like in the future.

External changes are also factors. The health care industry exemplifies a combination of the inability to predict the future with external changes. The health care industry is subject to an entirely new set of government regulations and an entirely new structure imposed from the national level. At the same time, technology is rapidly evolving for the delivery of health care services. This involves the quality, location, and the relationships between health care professionals and their patients. These changes have not been unexpected. These types of changes are, obviously, subject to all kinds of discomfort keys.

Discomfort Two: New Players Emerge

A second discomfort key is the emergence of new players. New firms come into an industry because they have redefined themselves. They come into a new industry because they are no longer doing what they did before. These firms have said to themselves, "We are not in the same business any more; we're a lot different." They enter new trade associations and industries; they become new players there. At that point, we begin to see some discontinuity, discomfort, and movement toward potential reorganization.

Discomfort Three: Predicting Survivors

There is a need to be able to predict who will survive in your industry and your marketplace. You need to know to whom you are going to deliver a set of services over the next five or ten years. You need to know for whom and for what you are in business. Every trade association that deals with financial institutions, for example, is in this position right now. That industry has gone through a decade of change. It undoubtedly will go through another decade of change. At the other end of the decade there will be certain survivors. The way that industry shapes up, and the nature of those survivors, is going to determine the needs a trade or professional organization will be expected to fill. Any doubt about the question of identifying survivors is one of the other areas of discomfort.

Discomfort Four: Change in Industry Concentration

Finally, increasing or decreasing concentration of industry—for example, a bi-polarization of an industry's structure into only mega organizations and very small niche players—represents a discomfort key. If they were large or small firms before, then they became even larger or smaller. Increasing concentration or polarization dictates a great need to be more flexible and more fluid in billing for services and products.

Now pause a moment and self-diagnose. Where is your organization, and what does your industry face based on the conditions described? The success of any reinvention effort actually begins in the design of the process used to literally recreate the organization.

Repositioning Case Study—From Office to Business Products

A case study is presented here examining the motivations for and processes of an association re-engineering for the office products industry. Compare which elements of this study are similar to those you may be experiencing. Which are significantly different?

Crisis and Discomfort in the Office Products Industry

Some of the significant changes that occurred in the office products industry can be tied to crisis and discomfort keys. The greatest crisis key this industry faced was technology change. Significant changes occurred that altered the delivery system of office products. Large retailers took over a significant portion of the marketplace.

There had been an unbelievable decrease in the number of small- and medium-sized office products dealers.

As mentioned earlier, the office products industry was a "mom and pop" operation but, as a number of huge office products supermarkets emerged, the number of total players in the retail segment dwindled dramatically. This represented another industry discomfort.

The two discomfort keys relevant to this case study were (1) the inability to predict the industry's structure for the future (because the whole structure of the industry was changing very rapidly making it impossible to predict what it was going to be like in two or three years, let alone five years), and (2) the emergence of new players. Significant new players in the industry changed the nature of the association. It also changed what those members wanted from the association.

Related to this shift, dealer groups were forming, and are still forming in the industry, responding to needs they have as individual firms. This also had a significant impact on the association—needs must be addressed within a buying group or a franchise system in terms of the kinds of products and services they expect the association or associations to provide for them.

In the office products industry there was a shift in industry power from the manufacturer to the consumer. Many industries have undergone this shift to focus on where the real power lies—with the consumer in the buying group—rather than with other segments of the industry. In this instance, it made a huge difference because, until now, manufacturers had been supporting multiple industry associations. As the power shift occurred, however, the resources for them to continue to do that were simply not available.

This caused considerable consolidation and vertical integration. It became increasingly difficult in this industry to define the segment in which a player belonged. Manufacturers changed distribution channels and became involved in distributing directly to retailers as well as to other distribution channels. That affected wholesale distribution and retailers involved in manufacture as well.

An increase in partnerships across segments took place—not only vertical integration but partnerships. In the manufacturing arena medium-sized manufacturers began to disappear; the large manufacturers and small niche ones became positioned to succeed. Such trends are apparent in a lot of other industries, perhaps even in your own.

Competition and Duplication Among Associations

Why, now, would the industry be interested in redesigning its association? In this case, there existed multiple industry associations competing for financial resources. Competition also existed, significantly, for the time key people in the industry could devote to association volunteer efforts. There were common members and common leaders in those associations. While companies were reluctant to say "We can't participate any longer in all these associations," they were hoping others would say it so they could then go along. That was the situation when the industry became interested in association redesign.

Along with substantial duplication of government and among individuals involved, the industry's associations were duplicating staff and programs and services. At the same time, data indicated there also existed significant gaps in programs and services. Needs were not being addressed to respond to changes occurring in the industry. The associations were fully aware of the changes going on in the industry. They were poorly positioned to respond quickly to those changes. By the time they could deliver products and services, needs disappeared.

Undertaking the Study

Industry leadership, although it initially had formed multiple associations, became interested in exploring some new kind of relationship or structure, some new way for the associations to serve the office products industry. They undertook an industry study, which, while not a study of a re-engineering of one particular association, might represent a different way for your industry to approach its problems.

The objectives of this study were fourfold:

1. The first objective was to figure out a better way to serve the needs of those in the industry. This placed a heavy emphasis on the issue of level of service as it related to future industry needs.
2. The second objective was to propose a future structure that could, in some way, be responsive to industry needs, based on the probable future structure. Remember, though, the associations were already having a hard time predicting what the industry would look like in the future.
3. The third objective was to keep industry participants informed. The study was to include a broad communications component so the rumor mill would not be the primary way people obtained information. This was an important effort and it was somewhat successful.

4. The fourth objective was to develop a specific transition plan to ensure that, in effecting recommended changes, member service disruption would be avoided. This is critically important to any kind of re-engineering.

Re-Engineering Phases

Notice the phases of re-engineering. There are three key processes: data collection, setting direction, and transition planning. There were four key elements of these processes:

1. The first is the issue of *key stakeholder participation*. Association leaders must be fully aware of the importance of involving key stakeholders in the process from the beginning. They should be involved, first, in the design of the project itself; second, as sources of information, initially in research and on an ongoing basis; third, in interpreting that information, developing alternative models, and then analyzing them; and, finally, in the ultimate decision-making.
2. The second element is *comprehensive data collection*. More and more work is taking place related to organizational issues and less related to pure strategic planning, perhaps because associations have moved along and do have strategic planning models now, but they still need to deal with organizational issues. Frequently situations develop where the re-engineering process stops on an organization-related issue because, although leaders have their own opinions and are willing to listen to the opinions of other participants, they have not been given enough data about how their members feel about what they (the leaders) perceive as a big risk. The only way to get around this is to give them really good data about what their members believe, how they feel, and what they perceive. Let that data be the basis on which decision makers together do good, productive thinking.
3. A third key element to the process is *some way of establishing consensus* among the leadership on vision—specific outcomes they are seeking to achieve. A set of guiding principles should be developed. A good level of consensus should be obtained on some of the key processes, on what the data says, and on the vision of what the organization will be like before moving into too much detail.
4. The fourth key element is *open communication*. In implementing the entire process and, particularly, in developing the transition plan, it is crucial that key leaders have a common vision. As they face the politics involved in the issue of multiple organizations, they need to be able to cope with threats they will feel from this kind of change. A framework must be established to which leaders can return and say, "Look, here is our vision, and that is what we're after; now how do we deal

with this little issue?" That is vitally important, and it depends on comprehensive, open communication so everyone is fully aware of what is going on.

Whatever the industry, leaders need a detailed needs assessment of it by segments to ascertain common needs and segment needs. This should include an analysis of each of the industry's participating associations identifying their strengths, weaknesses, and capabilities. Also needed is an assessment of their current programs and a look at how those are positioned relative to the programs and services provided by other associations. Then leaders will be in a position to consider the advantages of re-engineering.

Implementing Re-engineering

The second part of this case study is a substantive description of the nature of the organization that emerged from this work. It was formed by bringing together all these elements.

Future trends were anticipated, so the organization model that developed was designed not just to serve current problems, but to position the organization successfully for a future only somewhat foreseeable. A needs assessment was conducted, revealing, among other things, a consensus across all elements of the industry that things were not the way people wished them to be. They certainly were not prepared to meet future needs anticipated by a consensus of the industry. Perhaps, more than anything else, sharing the needs assessment/market research information created the consensus and critical mass among industry power influences that permitted change to occur.

Achieving "Buy In"

The often encountered conservative response, "I know these changes are happening; I do believe we should move in this direction, but would you do me a favor? Would you just leave things alone for another five years until I'm out of here?" was mitigated by recognizing that the dynamics of the industry were not going to remain static for those five years. Probing more deeply, it was discovered, the individual was saying, "Leave things alone for five years. I'm at a certain age; my business is at a certain point; I just want to recapture the equity I put into it. I'm going to sell it or turn it over to somebody else." Our reply was fact-based: "You can make that judgment now as a leader in this association, but we cannot guarantee to you that, without these changes, you will have a business to sell in five years." Those traditional objections were overcome, but only because of the presence of defensible information.

The impact of this statement could be seen on the industry's associations. It was critical to achieve "buy-in," not merely from the staff leadership of existing associations, but from the partnership that existed between elected and staff leadership. Resistance driven by staff members' desires to preserve status, situations, and income, was offset by recognizing that even the position of leader of an association in a declining industry was, itself, in jeopardy. This overcame a natural resistance to critical change.

The New Structure

Current conditions of the industry and its associations were presented parallel to a recommended position. This picture of the present conditions of the industry associations depicted competition for financial resources; duplication of governing staff, programs, and services; perceived lapses in programs and services; fragmented goals and purposes; slow responses to changing industry conditions; and traditional work force structures. The picture of desirable conditions depicted a single, unified association; a strategic alliance among industry segments; governance and staff focusing on meeting industry needs; program decisions based on continuous needs assessment research; direction setting based on formal strategic planning; rapid response based on information and knowledge; and a flexible work force combining volunteers, core staff, contracting services, and temporary workers.

There was a dramatic contrast between existing conditions and what could be or should be. The development process then focused attention and energy, not on protecting the traditions of the past but, instead, on what needed to happen to move the organization and the industry it served to what it could be. Re-focusing energy from a defensive position based on past experience to careful consideration of where it wanted to be created a dramatic change in the dynamic of the development process.

For industries in transition, moving toward unification with a different power distribution, such as occurs in traditional models of federation or aggregation through mergers (which are really acquisitions), simply would not work for this industry. The usual approach to redistributing power on a larger number of groups is not effective in any industry experiencing rapid and unpredictable change.

This is why that is the case. If power is redistributed in the old, traditional formats, you formalize and end up with a picture of the inside of a bucket you can tip over. If the structure of the industry is dramatically changing and you glue down onto the page the redistribution of power that you achieved at the moment you made the transition, it is only a short period of time before you are facing the same problem again.

A unified organization was needed with the ability, built right into the structural design, to automatically and smoothly redistribute power as the industry changed. This relieves the professional staff of an enormous emotional and political burden. Staff no longer has to advocate constant change in the distribution of power among the volunteer leadership force. Built into the process is the automatic adjustment of that power.

Strategic Business Sections

The term used to describe the elements or parts of this organization was "strategic business section" or "strategic business segment (SBS)." These generic terms were chosen because they were unlike any labels previously used in associations of this type. This signaled these sections were not traditional special interest groups, divisions, or councils. Their role was different; the nature of their work was different; how they came to be and how they come to be undone, over time, would also be different. This label would also be appropriate for the language and jargon of the industry, since members of this organization were, in many instances, leaders of corporate environments and cultures.

It was recommended that the various industry associations become strategic sections or groups, placed under a single umbrella of a core organization. They would operate as quasi-independent associations but under guidelines defined by the core organization, which was driven by the conditions of the marketplace. This is one of the essential differences between this new model and the prior structure of the associations. The structure, process, and program of the organization would be driven by changes in needs, expectations, and industry structure. This new relationship increased fluidity.

Let us make this more tangible. What would the picture of such an organization look like? Figure 9 shows an organizational chart different from what most people are probably used to. It is a series of concentric circles with different levels of the circles divided into different parts like a pie. The center of the circles is the corporate core. Specific functions are assigned to it that involve things the group servicing the unified segments is strategically better positioned to accomplish than any of the individual segments.

Strategic capacity and position is another essential element defining this model. Judgments about how to organize the new association were not premised on who controlled what, but on what level and part of the organization had the capacity and strategic position, the knowledge, the leverage point, and the political wherewithal to accomplish certain things best.

The Corporate Core

The corporate core was led by a board of directors whose primary responsibility was policy. The board of directors was kept relatively small, about fifteen to twenty people. Within the board of directors was a subgroup of four or five people called the executive committee. The primary responsibility of the executive committee was overseeing the operations of the organization. This was very different from the past experience and structure of the organizations that were now part of the reinvention.

We sought to compress the decision-making process and increase the organization's flexibility so it could quickly reallocate assets as required by changes in members' needs. This meant literally pushing down, not just one level, but two levels of authority that traditionally had been distributed through the predecessor organizations. To support what we did, responsibilities and authorities previously vested in a membership organization or meeting were pushed down to a board of directors half the size of any former board.

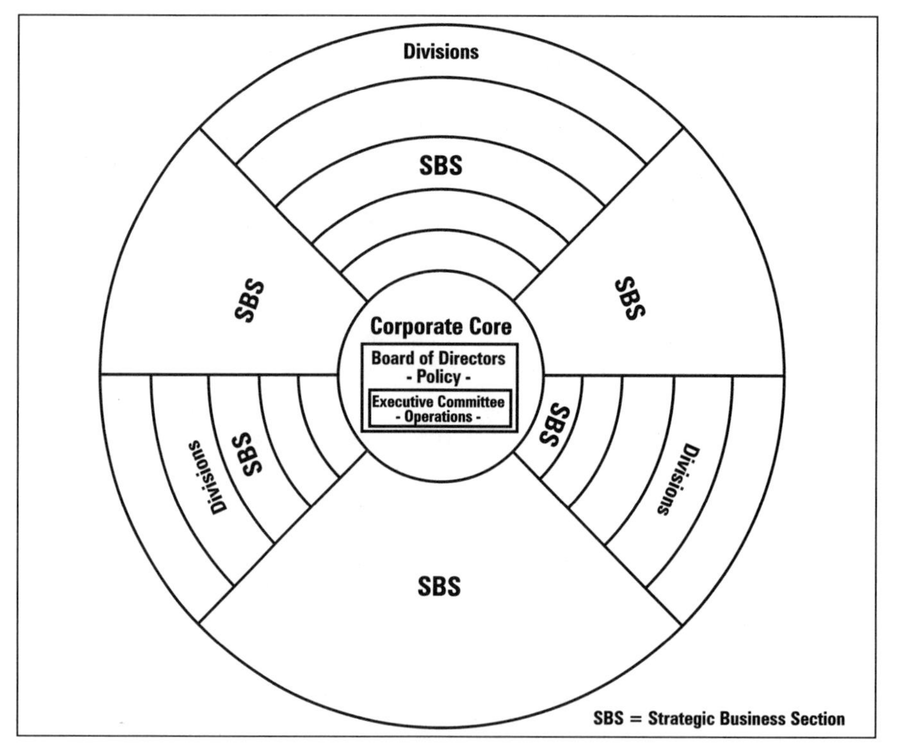

Figure 9. Organization Structure: United Office Products Industry Association

The previous authorities and responsibilities of the board of directors then were pushed down to an executive committee one-third the size of any such previous group. Just as important, the responsibilities and authorities that in most association models were customarily vested in an executive committee or officers were pushed directly onto the staff. Among other things, one of the effects of this change was that this organization would soon have committees and members advising staff.

Critical to the re-design was who possessed expertise. This was considered every bit as important as where authority needed to be vested politically. This caused the model to be more businesslike and less government-like in the way it dealt with organization politics.

Surrounding the corporate core was a series of business sections, each representing a different segment of the industry. A strategic business section could create itself any time some new combination, either through vertical or horizontal aggregation of the industry, created a new group of needs, expectations, and personalities. Conversely, when a strategic business section lost its ability to attract sufficient membership or lost its ability to provide a program sufficiently attractive to a large enough group, it would literally melt away. Its purposes would devolve to other places in the organization. A fundamental characteristic of the new organization structure was that it depended on members to approve program benefits being provided. This was a dramatic shift in norm and culture.

Each of the strategic business sections was able to subdivide itself further into divisions. In some cases, they represented smaller groups of common self-interest within a segment of the industry whose members just liked to spend time together.

The board of directors of the new model organization is responsible for providing policy guidelines for forming these subgroups and for providing them information. That is part of policy. These guidelines, though, should be broad and general. They constitute a set of criteria that determines when sufficient critical mass has been reached to create a strategic business section.

We wanted to make sure this model did not totally abandon or deflate existing values and traditions of the organization. Abandoning old values and attacking existing traditions creates unnecessary defensive opposition. To the extent possible, the model was made sufficiently permeable so that present players would feel comfortable becoming part of this new way of getting work delivered. Many of these SBSs would even become individual associations later, serving different industry segments.

Not for Everyone

It would be wrong to imply that instant, unanimous agreement should be expected in a change of this magnitude. All the existing associations did not decide to become parts of a new model. In one case, the group was headed by a management company that saw no benefit in dissolving its contract. In a second instance, there was a rather well-endowed senior staff person who also saw no self-benefit in devolving into the organization yet.

Membership in this unified association could be in three major components. First, each member firm of an organization would be a general member and would then be able, if they chose, to become a member of any of the strategic business segments. They did not have to meet any defining criteria to be eligible to join a segment.

Open Marketplace Approach

This model attempts, to the greatest extent possible, to encourage the organization to abandon its traditional role as a rule maker. Associations, particularly their staffs, have always spent tremendous amounts of energy creating rules and making people follow them. Our research and experience tells us that members are no longer interested associations doing this. Members would prefer that energy be directed from the role of rule enforcer to the roles of consultant and service provider. This new model left it to members to decide in which segment they wished to invest time and money.

The dynamic described here is an open marketplace approach within the association, compatible with the industry marketplace. The association reflects industry dynamics. This industry's solution represents an illustration of a knowledge-based approach.

What has really happened here? Remember that the office supply industry was an industry that had been a collection of "mom and pop" installations. Suddenly, almost overnight, came Staples, OfficeMax, BusMart, Office Depot, and other superstores. The office supply industry association, literally, had no capacity and no structural opportunity for such large entities to become part of it. None of the existing associations were suitable homes for this changing industry. The power in the industry was evolving into another kind of organization that simply had no place to go. The question was, could we give it a home or would these firms develop their own homes together, thereby creating a competitor organization?

In this new model, each strategic business group determines its own organizational and governance structure. Abandonment of the traditional role of rule-maker is reflected in the degree of autonomy provided each group. The only way to empower a group to decide quickly enough what is required to respond to members' evolving needs is to give it the ability to do so without checking with somebody else. This still must be balanced with the need for strategic coherency in the overall direction an association is supporting for the industry as a whole.

Governance

The board of directors, therefore, was constructed so it represented all the members and served as a policy-making body of the organization. This produced the condition where each subpart of the organization focused on programs while the core focused on policy. This is another major difference between this model and other models of association organization found among federations, collaboratives, functional affiliations, and similar groups. In this instance, small groups, or work groups, are designed to focus on programs; that is where their energy goes as opposed to positioning themselves as active participants in the power process of the organization.

This, along with using formal strategic planning or research, here called "needs assessment," and an interactive budgeting process, took the leadership of the organization out of the traditional power politics of an evolving industry and, instead, allowed it to be much more businesslike, focusing on providing service and opportunity. Committing to flexibility, re-focusing on programs rather than power, using ongoing needs assessment to maintain currency in program and policy initiatives, abandoning walls between silos—these design decisions reflected the industry's decision to move toward knowledge-based culture in a new, unified industry association.

Knowledge-Based: A Marketplace Model

Specifications for programs were broad, but clear. Programs and services common to all the segments were to be developed by the corporate association, the core. Programs and services uniquely attractive to one or another segment are the responsibility of those particular segments. They are developed only by the core if enough different parts of the industry are interested or if the core is better positioned to do it well.

How would decisions be made as to whether the segment or the core should handle particular programs? Because "knowledge based" means that content and process expertise in making necessary decisions is available, who made the decision became an issue of less consequence than the quality of the decision.

Here are those four basic questions again. Because they are basic to understanding how this model is knowledge based, they cannot be repeated too often.

- Question one: What do we know about the members' needs, wants, and delivery preferences, segment by segment, relative to this decision?

- Question two: What do we know about the capacity and strategic position of this organization and each business segment within it relative to this decision?
- Question three: What do we know about the current realities and evolving dynamics of our members' marketplace relevant to this decision?
- Question four: What are the ethical implications of the choices we make?

The third of the four questions, which relates to the current realities and evolving dynamics of the memberships' marketplace, moves the organization toward being more market-directed. This is one of the suggested characteristics of the evolving decision process. "Market-directed" means the organization is reaching, through members, information about members' customer populations.

Needs assessment, strategic planning process, and the various data collection technologies that are the essential sources of knowledge for decision making are the responsibility of the corporate core. The corporate core is a service provider to the various parts of the organization.

This extends the marketplace model one more important step. The segments of the organization view the corporate core as a primary provider of services they need to do their jobs well. If they do not get what they want from the corporate core, or if they think they can get a better deal somewhere else, in this model they are encouraged to go outside the organization for the service.

This creates a shared accountability and an interdependence among all the parts so that even the corporate core must remain responsive to its internal marketplace. If it does not, it will quickly see signs that indicate it is not delivering. People will be reaching somewhere else to get the support and functional services they want. A knowledge-based enterprise is well positioned to continue to earn its members' allegiance on an ongoing basis.

Decisions about continuing existing programs are based on a formal, strategic, program assessment. Strategic program assessment is a particular analysis that allows an organization to make decisions about the future of a program more rationally. It assesses a given program and determines to what extent it is related to the mission and goals of the organization. To what extent is it a good investment for the future? Decisions about each program's future are more rationally based in this model. They are based less on emotions and power. These are things more government-like and less businesslike decision processes tend to be based on.

Finances

SBSs may collaborate on developing joint programs and services. Program responsibilities, again, are clarified by the board through policy. All members pay general dues and pay additionally to belong to a segment. General dues support corporate and essential services, and each segment determines whether additional dues are charged to support its own activities and programs. All money flows to the corporate core and from the corporate core out. This model will not work if money flows to the subparts, and then the subparts send their money to the core.

Flexible Work Force

In a knowledge-based organization the work force needs to be flexible. It needs to treat volunteers, core staff, contracted services, and temporary workers all as partners, each providing a different kind of service. A reporting relationship exists so collaboration among the sections is naturally built into the organization's dynamics. It is obviously in the best interests of each segment's general manager to find collaborative partners with whom to develop and provide programs.

Figure 10 illustrates this. This four-leaf clover design treats different groupings as equal partners providing capacity in different ways to the organization. This is not a hierarchy; it is more like a collaborative network. This model provides cost-effective flexibility in allocating resources in a traumatically evolving environment.

Our experience and observation discloses two things: One, associations cannot depend on members as primary sources for useful information. Members know very clearly what they want; very few of them know what they need. There are two reasons: (1) they do not understand what associations are well positioned to do, so they do not know what is on the menu, let alone how to pick the best thing; (2) they really do not understand their marketplace to the same degree as individuals who devote all of their attention to studying the market rather than just serving it.

What is needed is a variety of technologies that will allow associations to constantly amass and provide information that accurately describes the evolution and current condition of the marketplace. More simply put, if we know what consumers are looking for and find desirable, that helps the organization determine what and how it needs to serve its members.

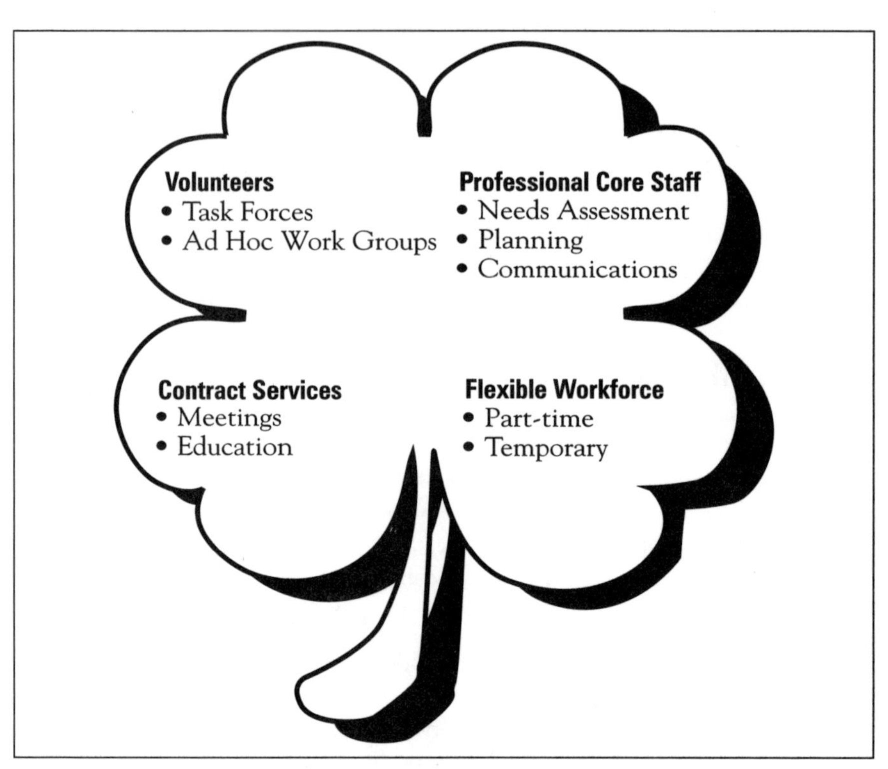

Figure 10. Four Leaf Clover Model of Staffing Structure—United Office Products Industry Association

Market Research Tools

There are a variety of research tools that can provide that information. These, though, must be routinely and explicitly budgeted. Market and marketing research must become a function of the organization, not just a project or an event. Its applications include focus group research, telephone interviews, psychodemographic analysis, actually observing consumer behavior, and using evolving technologies for bar-coding and tracking actual consumer behavior on the spot. This might include video gridding consumers' movement through a store to yield information reflecting actual behavior, not just somebody's opinion. Those are some of the kinds of technologies available—the last one is extremely exciting.

Supermarkets, for some time now, have had access to three national data bases that automatically provide a tremendous depth of information the moment somebody passes an item across the cashier's scanner. The buying habits of individuals are now being collectively tracked. They are being aggregated, and members of certain associations in that industry, by virtue of their membership, may access that data base. That, by the way, as you might imagine, is considered an enormous membership benefit. The knowledge-based model is designed to focus attention on those kinds of twenty-first century, information-intensive benefits.

A number of associations in several industries, including health care, produce, finance, banking and insurance, office products, and telecommunications, are beginning to move toward implementing this approach. Because it is truly a new model, there is still no organization, to our knowledge, which has fully implemented it.

Here is another caveat. The knowledge-based model itself suggests implementation will never be totally complete. It is designed to create a dynamic organization for providing service in an ongoing, similarly dynamic environment. That is one of the big differences between this model and others. Several organizations, including the National Association of Realtors and the Produce Marketing Association, are making significant progress in this direction.

Relentless change, and change in the nature and rate of change itself, is causing the environments of industries and professions and their related organizations to become unstable and unpredictable. Under such circumstances, it is logical and, in many instances, necessary for industry and organization leaders to reassess their association structures, efficiency, and effectiveness to keep up with the requirements and needs of their memberships. The new, unified, flexible, information-based, market-directed, needs-oriented, knowledge-based organization model emerges as a sensible and practical solution for the challenges of the times.

Constructing Strategic Alliances or Consolidations

One paradox of the twenty-first century is that, increasingly, cooperation is a competitive strategy of choice. While associations are different than for-profit enterprises, similar movements in the not-for-profit sector reinforce the attraction of cooperation as a choice. This occurs even in industries with a history of strong competition. In a for-profit enterprise the job is to find the need and to be the one that fills it. If a for-profit corporation does not do that, it has got a problem.

The role of an association, however, is very different. Its job is to find the need and make sure that it gets met, not necessarily to be the entity that meets it. Sometimes creating a strategic alliance with a competitor (there are many different forms of them) is actually in the best strategic interests of the association. It allows each of the allies to focus resources on the things they do best by shedding commitments to things the other is better positioned to do. Members' needs can be met with superlative quality as a result of this ability to focus.

By creating alliances with competitors you can acquire greater depth in what you do in exchange for sacrificing breadth by giving up those things you do, at best, only in mediocre fashion. Associations, now, are reaching out to each other and other kinds of private and public partners and creating a variety of strategic alliances from consolidation to collaboration, cooperation, and coordination.

The strategies differ. Sometimes they are mergers, sometimes acquisitions. Many times an acquisition masquerades as a merger to be politically palatable. In a knowledge-based association, it is an attempt by the organization to clarify and focus its service niche.

In a knowledge-based association, decisions about relationships, as well as structure, program, and process, are better informed. The myriad of choices on the continuum from competition to consolidation—coordination, cooperation, collaboration, strategic alliance, and joint venture—are better understood and more rationally considered.

CHAPTER 15

Final Words: Teaching an Elephant to Dance

A few years ago James Belasco wrote a book called, "Teaching the Elephant to Dance" (1991). It was a treatise on moving big organizations, and it raised two important questions. One was, "Why in the world would you want an elephant to dance when there are so many other kinds of things you can more easily get to dance? Why not a poodle or a person?"

The second question was, "Did anybody ask the elephant?" Elephants tend not to want to dance. When they try to dance, they do not do it very well, so what you get is a ticked-off elephant.

The point is that change in your environments, your member constituencies, and their needs and desires, along with technology hurtling us into the future, is creating a time when your elephant will have to learn to dance. It will be dancing to the music of the future, and the band of the twenty-first century will be playing. You will need persistence and skill to recognize your organization's pressure points to make the necessary changes as painless and effective as possible. This will be required to achieve success in coming years.

Scenes from the Road

Although we know of no organization that has fully completed it, there are many associations that have begun the journey toward becoming knowledge based. Our initial observations suggest several key points:

1. *The path is not the same for everyone—every organization manifests the elements differently*. No two associations are likely to respond to the dynamics of change in exactly the same way. Conditions unique to the industry, profession, or issue arena with which the organization is involved are likely to require a customized solution. The history and organizational peculiarities of each association will likely require a carefully conceived strategy for managing through change.
2. *All steps can't be completed in sequential order*. Many must be done in a parallel way, such as addressing culture and climate throughout the journey.
3. *Most organizations embarking on the journey are finding ways to escape an internally driven, short-term view in favor of a longer-range, externally focused view*. Significant

culture change, which can rarely be facilitated from within, is being aided by being able to look outside the organization itself.

The tools, systems, strategies, and approaches successful associations are at least experimenting with, if not employing, may or may not be useful to you. You must still do your own thinking about what will and will not work in your own environment and adapt it accordingly. In truth, in association management, as the twenty-first century approaches, there is no one best answer for anything. This stark reality is a fundamental assumption in a knowledge-based operational philosophy employing informed intuition as its style of decision making.

Starting Now

The core of the knowledge-based operational philosophy is a commitment to a different value system. This value system stands on the premise that who makes the decision is far less important than the quality of information and insight on which the decision is made.

The cursor is moving further away from the political model of decision making and closer to a more business- or information-based model. There is no switch that can be thrown to jump from one model to another; this represents a subtle transition and shifting of focus.

Being knowledge based stands for a lot more than just that. In an association engaged in the journey toward the consultative partnership, everything else in the organization tends to change as well. It is much too soon for anyone to really know what the association community will become over the next twenty-five years.

We all depend on associations with a tradition of continually finding and developing new tools and solutions to meet demands forever evolving. However, each association's willingness to reshape itself for a more knowledge-based future will likely determine its ability to successfully evolve in the twenty-first century.

References

Belasco, James. 1991. *Teaching the elephant to dance*. New York: Plume Publishing.

Foundation of the American Society of Association Executives. 1995. Environmental scan. Unpublished report. Washington, D.C.

Senge, Peter. 1990. *The fifth discipline—The art and practice of the learning organization*. New York: Doubleday.

Tapscott, Dan. 1996. *The digital economy: Promise and peril in the age of networked intelligence*. New York: McGraw-Hill.

Tecker, Glenn, and Marybeth Fidler. 1993. *Successful association leadership: Dimensions of 21st century competency for the* CEO. Washington, D.C.: ASAE Foundation.

About the Authors

Glenn H. Tecker is president and chief executive officer of Tecker Consultants, Trenton, New Jersey, an international consulting firm specializing in management, education, and organization. He has served as an association executive and as a board member for both not-for-profit and private sector organizations. He has assisted a wide variety of trade, professional, and philanthropic organizations in the redesign of governance, program, and operations in order to more effectively navigate through today's rapidly shifting environments. His other published works for ASAE include *Successful Association Leadership: Dimensions of 21st Century Competency for the* CEO, and the *Association Education Handbook.*

Kermit M. Eide is a principal partner of Tecker Consultants. He works with a wide variety of national, state, and local trade and professional associations in meeting such challenges as creating vision; re-focusing on core principles, values, and purpose; reshaping culture, processes, and structures; and planning for the future. He spent a number of years in public education and held management positions in education, strategic planning, and organizational consulting with AT&T.

Jean S. Frankel is a principal partner of Tecker Consultants. She has assisted associations with strategic planning, organizational redesign, leadership development, and the use of technology to achieve organizational improvement. She has held management and consulting positions at major corporations such as American Express and AT&T and has now focused her practice exclusively on strategic and organizational planning for associations. She is a frequent speaker on organizational strategy and technology integration at association conferences and symposiums.